# Did I Say That?

# Did I Say That?

## by John L. McKenzie

The Thomas More Press

The material in this book appeared in different form in *The Critic* magazine, published by the Thomas More Association, 180 N. Wabash Ave.,
Chicago, Ill. 60601

Standard Book Number 0–88347–026–8

# CONTENTS

*Chapter One*

# THE STATE IN CHRISTIAN PERSPECTIVE

OSCAR CULLMAN once wrote that interest in the problem of church and state usually becomes vital only when open conflict between the two arises. He could have added that open conflict does not create an atmosphere favorable to clear thinking. A heated dispute is not directed to the discovery and exposition of the truth but rather to a defensive statement of convictions which are maintained all the more firmly because they are threatened. Cullman's remark had reference to the European theological discussion which was set off by the rise of National Socialism in Germany. In this discussion, as Rudolf Schnackenburg noted, Catholics took little part. If European Catholics were not engaged, American Catholics were even less concerned. There has not been a genuine church-state conflict in this country since the signing of the Constitution. Here there has been and still is an atmosphere in which scholars could think on the question without feeling a compulsion to take a defensive position. The unfinished work of John Courtney Murray is a splendid example of constructive thinking; the fact that his work is unfinished shows that the defensive attitude still exists.

Murray's work at least made it clear that there is no "Catholic" thesis on the question in the proper sense of the term. The political-ethical theses which have been maintained, and

9

some of which have become conventional, are based on the historical acts of the church, theoretically justified by philosophical reasoning. There is no theological thesis of the relations of church and state; and "theological" here, like "Catholic" above, is used in the proper and rigorous sense. This is a simple statement of fact with no implications that a theological thesis cannot be reached. No thesis, either philosophical or theological, is intended here, nor any argument directed against any existing thesis. I intend a simple inquiry into what the New Testament has to say about the problem.

The inquiry is not easy, but the work done by scholars permits one to pass over some points quickly. The discussion carried on in Europe reached no consensus; the texts permit one to find in the New Testament a positive affirmation of the values of the state, a negative rejection of the state, and a neutral position. The discussion also permits one to say that the problem, if its urgency is judged by the number of texts which can be adduced as directly pertinent, is not an urgent problem in the New Testament. It permits one to say also that one must be very cautious in forming generalizations from the New Testament texts, which reflect a concrete historical situation. And here two conditions in which the New Testament texts must be considered should be mentioned.

The first condition is that the New Testament did not arise in a vacuum; here as elsewhere we look for the background of thought in which the New Testament was composed, and here as elsewhere we look at the Old Testament and Judaism. "Thought" is hardly the correct word for what we find about the state in the Old Testament, but fortunately the material can be summed up briefly. The Old Testament knows only two states: the monarchies of Israel and Judah in one group, and all other states together. Israel is submitted to God; all other states are not in submission. Other states are granted power by God; they are the rod of his anger, like Assyria (Is. 10:5), or the earth is given into their hands, like Nebuchadnezzar of Babylon (Jer. 27). When this happens, to resist them is to resist God himself. But they are unbelieving and godless, and all of them will ultimately perish in the judgments of God. The Old Testament sees no enduring society of men living in peace and order until the reign of God is firmly and finally established. Man cannot build an enduring society; the Old Testament goes immediately from historical states to the eschatological reign.

The second condition is the concrete historical situation of the New Testament. The New Testament knows nothing of "the state" in the abstract. The only state it knows is Rome; and Rome was a superstate, effectively a world state. It was very nearly as much a part of existence as the atmosphere. We cannot talk about the New Testament teaching on the state; we can talk only of the New Testament's attitude toward Rome, and we can make extended generalizations as far as our generalization corresponds to the historical reality of Rome. A synthesis of church-Rome relationships may and indeed ought to be the foundation of a synthesis of church-state relationships, but the two are not identical. This is important precisely because Rome was a world state; not only was there nothing with which to compare it, there was also no known alternative to chaos and barbarism. To this we shall return.

There are only two sayings of Jesus which have any direct reference to the state: the answer of Jesus to the question about the tribute and the answer to Pilate concerning the nature of the kingship of Jesus. The more one thinks about the words, "Render to Caesar the things that are Caesar's, and to God the things that are God's" (Mk. 12:17; Mt. 22:21; Lk. 22:25), the more one suspects that they are not the answer to the question but a refusal to answer. Jesus cannot possibly have divided man's allegiance between God and Caesar. If God's claims are total—and nothing else is conceivable—can Caesar have any claims? The obscurity of the answer has elicited a massive literature of interpretation, none of which is satisfying. One can only conclude that God does not exact tribute, and that tribute is due to him in whose coinage the tribute is paid. Tribute was and is an acknowledgement of submission. The acceptance of a political authority does not of itself take anything away from what is due to God. The saying implies nothing about the right of the ruler to exact tribute, which is precisely the question asked; and this is why I believe that Jesus refused to answer. Instead of a *de jure* answer, he treated the question *de facto*. The fact was that the Jews were governed by Caesar and there was nothing they could do about it. If they used his money, he could get their tribute. By what means or in what quantity or by what right—these questions are not answered. We may conjecture that to Jesus they were not important. What he taught that man could be and do did not depend on Caesar. Caesar had to be accepted as a fact—like the atmosphere, as I have observed. Like the weather, he might be good or bad; but for the end which Jesus presented, he could be ignored.

The second saying of Jesus which bears on the state is his answer to Pilate's question about his kingship. Jesus affirms that he is a king, but that his kingdom is not of or from this world (Jn. 18:36-37). This is a clear disclaimer of any political involvement, and Pilate took it in this sense; whatever Pilate's skepticism about the truth, he understood at once that the case of Jesus did not fall under his jurisdiction. While this dialogue is missing in the Synoptic Gospels, they likewise tell that Pilate at first admitted no guilt in Jesus.

This is an answer and not a refusal to answer; but the answer is in line with the saying about tribute paid to Caesar. Jesus denies that the government has any reason to be concerned with him; he also denies that he has any concern with the government. No relationship is assumed or hinted; no union, no separation, no concordat—in short, no problem. Jesus and Caesar, to borrow a phrase from the text itself, move in different worlds. Neither contributes to the other; neither owes anything to the other. And this was perceived at once by an administrator who probably did not reach the level of the best men in the foreign service of Rome.

We can add a third saying of Jesus, although it does not touch the state directly. Jesus demands that his followers should not behave like those who lord it over the Gentiles and exercise authority over them; whoever is great among his followers must be the slave of all (Mk. 10:42-44; Mt. 20:25-27; Lk. 22:25-27). This saying is not hostile to the state; neither is it friendly. There will be authority and subjects in the company of the followers of Jesus; but the exercise of the authority must have no resemblance to secular government. Positively, the one who holds authority is the slave of others, but not their master. This is certainly a new conception of authority. It leaves no room in the church for anything resembling the secular government of the ancient world; this is scarcely an endorsement of secular government as a part of the Christian way of life.

In the last exchange between Jesus and Pilate which John records, Jesus says that Pilate has his power over Jesus from above (Jn. 19:11). I defer any discussion of this text until we come to Paul's text in Romans 13. For the moment we may notice that in the context of the Passion narrative and of the other sayings of Jesus, the text would never stand as a support for the divine right of Caesar. This reservation should be recalled when the text of Romans 13 is examined.

The scattered allusions to the state in the New Testament outside the Gospels are likewise few and almost entirely casual; but a pattern can be distinguished. When Paul sees Christ delivering the kingdom to the Father after destroying every rule and authority and power (I Cor. 15:24), he foresees the survival of no state in the eschatological kingdom. If marriage does not survive in the resurrection (Mk. 12:25; Mt. 22:30; Lk. 20:35), neither does the less personal and less intimate society of the state. Paul here echoes the Old Testament and Judaism, mentioned above; no human society survives the judgment of God, and the eschatological reign of God leaves no room for any merely human power. The state is clearly one of the features of "this world" which has no lasting reality.

Similarly, the transitory nature of the state is implied in Philippians 3:20 and Hebrews 13:14. Paul assures the Philippians that their *politeuma* is in heaven. This is an extremely interesting choice of words. *Politeuma* is as near the English word *state* as any Greek word; but in usage it most frequently designates a colony of foreign residents. The implications are clear. The

Christian is never identified with the state as other citizens are. From the citizens and peoples of the Roman Empire, Rome demanded supreme loyalty; and this loyalty was sanctioned by a religious motif, the cult of the divine Caesar. The supreme loyalty of the Christian was to the reign of God, present in the church and moving toward the eschatological consummation. The author of Hebrews writes in the same line of thought when he says that we have not here a lasting city but seek the one that is coming (13:14). In the Hellenistic-Roman world, the city, the Polis, was the focus of civilized living. Every man had his Polis or ought to have, without which he was homeless and rootless. The Christian, too, has his Polis which gives him home and identity; but it is the eschatological Polis of the reign of God.

Paul would not have the Christians of Corinth recur to the government even in the ordinary and useful service of the courts of law (1 Cor. 6:1-8). In a genuine Christian community, no disputes which demand a judicial decision ought to arise at all; the Christian would yield before the dispute reaches that point. But Paul is realist enough to know that disputes will arise; if they do, they should be settled out of court by agreement reached within the Christian community, and not be referred to the unrighteous and the unbeliever. The Christian transformation, Paul certainly thinks, should make laws and courts unnecessary; and what would this leave for the state to do?

It seems that the texts mentioned so far can be classified as neutral in their attitude toward the state—remembering that "the state" is always the concrete historical state of Rome. We now turn to some texts in which the attitude is clearly hostile. These texts are not numerous; they are all found in the Apocalypse. Rome is the Beast (Apoc. 13) and the Great Whore of Babylon (Apoc. 17), who will be destroyed by God's avenging judgments (Apoc. 18). As in the Old Testament, the overthrow of the world power issues in the eschatological reign of God (Apoc. 19-22). The change of tone from the other New Testament writings is evident, and the explanation of the change of tone is evident also. The Apocalypse was written after the church had experienced persecution under Nero and Domitian.

Rome could no longer be simply ignored as having no relevance to the proclamation of the Gospel and the establishment of the church. It had become an enemy and subject to judgment; and the Apocalypse draws on the apocalyptic imagery of the Old Testament and Judaism to portray this judgment in vivid terms.

To arrange the texts as I have done could be considered slanting the evidence. But it may help to understand how Hans Windisch could have written that Romans 13:1-7 is a foreign body in the New Testament. This passage is in all probability the source of other passages in which the same friendly attitude toward Rome is exhibited (1 Pet. 2:13-17; 1 Tim. 2:1-2; Tit. 3:1). Here Paul proposes subjection to "the powers that be" for conscience' sake, payment of taxes, respect and honor to those to whom respect and honor are due. These recommendations do not go beyond the neutral attitude found elsewhere; but the basis on which Paul argues is novel. Obedience is due to authority because all authority is instituted by God; authority is the minister of God for the good of those who are ruled, and the agent of the wrath of God on the wrongdoer.

One feels a certain uneasiness when this passage is compared not only with the texts of the Gospel, but especially when it is compared with 1 Corinthians 6:1-8. There is no open contradiction, but there is a difference of mood and attitude. The exegetical controversies of recent years have revolved around the problem of whether Paul here gives Rome a positive value which it does not have elsewhere in the New Testament. If he does, the positive value consists in the position of Rome as an authority instituted by God and empowered to act as the minister of God's judgments "for your good." Does this establish the divine right of the state to rule?

Before one makes the affirmative answer which seems too obvious, one has to set this passage in the context of thought in which Paul lived. And the first element is the neutrality toward the state found in the sayings of Jesus. The second element is the Old Testament idea of the foreign state as the agent of God's judgments. What the prophets say of the state with reference to Israel is here said by Paul with reference to the individual criminal. The divine right of the state is no more clearly affirmed in one case than it is in the other. If one who resisted Nebuchadnezzar could be said by Jeremiah to resist God, so one who resists Rome could be said by Paul to resist God. That the power is given to Rome by God must be understood in biblical terms; and in biblical terms there is only one being possessed of power, and that is God. All power is derived from him, granted by him; but in biblical terms this does not establish the agent who receives power as either good or bad. Is Rome as the agent of God's wrath any better or worse than Assyria as the agent of God's wrath? In the wide view of biblical thought, there is no contradiction whatever between Paul's words in Romans 13 and what is written in the Apocalypse. The Beast and the Great Whore do not cease to be the minister of God's judgment; nor do they cease to be authorities instituted by God. Jesus, we have noticed, attributes to God the power which Pilate has over his life. Paul's conception of power does not differ. And here we turn up an important idea in the biblical conception of the state which is not at first apparent: the Bible never discusses what we could call the justice or the legitimacy of a government. If it exists, it is a power; and if it is a power it has received power from God, because it could not get power from any other source. To this we shall have to return.

A number of recent writers have looked for an explanation of Paul's thought in Romans 13 in the idea of the angels of the nations; this idea appears in Daniel 10:13, 20 and in the apocalyptic literature of Judaism.

These are not the conventional "angels" of Christian art and devotion; they are cosmic beings whose scope and power is, to put it delicately, ambiguous, and neither angelic nor demonic is the precise word for them. The power of the nations is mediated to them by God through these cosmic beings. Most interpreters have refused to see an allusion to this belief in Romans 13, and it is perhaps better not to lean on it too heavily, in spite of the fact that allusions to cosmic powers are sufficiently numerous in the Pauline writings. But with or without the cosmic beings, the view shows us how Paul fits the power of the state into his scheme. The state—and it is especially easy to conceive of the world state of Rome in this way—is one of the cosmic powers, a part of the structure of the material universe. Like all such powers, it is instituted by God and is his agent. Like all such powers, it can exhibit demonic traits at times. But one does not fight the state any more than one would fight the weather; and this attitude gives the state precisely that positive moral value which the weather has, no more and no less. The state is a part of the condition of human existence. If the state is so conceived, Paul's words in Romans 13 fall into harmony with the words of Jesus and of Paul himself elsewhere. The state remains indifferent in the Christian way of life.

If this is the correct understanding of Romans 13—and for such a difficult passage probability is all one can invoke in one's favor—then we can synthesize New Testament thought in a form in which it does not appear in the New Testament. The controlling factor is the sayings of Jesus. His words, as I have already suggested, nearly ignore the state. There is not the slightest indication that he conceived political means for the advancement of the church. The state can neither help nor hinder the Gospel. The Christian lives in a state as he lives in a climate; neither makes any difference to his Christian profession. Whether the state is one state or another is likewise irrelevant. I use this word, which some may find too strong, because I can find nothing in the words of Jesus which tells me how to form a judgment on these matters. Render to Caesar what is his; Jesus does not tell me to examine Caesar's credentials and to measure him against an abstract standard of law and justice. And if Jesus made no distinction between a just government and an unjust government, I see four conclusions which can be drawn from his silence: (1) All governments are equally just; (2) No government is just; (3) It makes no difference whether the government is just; (4) The word "just" is meaningless when applied to government. No one of these conclusions fits into our patterns of thought. Shall we tailor the words of Jesus to fit our patterns, or shall we revise our patterns?

That the New Testament contains no theology or philosophy of the state does not imply that we should have none. The New Testament has no theory of the movement of vehicular traffic either, but we are not unfaithful to the Gospel when we devise theories. But we are better aware of the relative importance of the values we deal with; we cast no halo of religious value over right-handed rather than left-handed roadways. The New Testament, I have emphasized, is historically conditioned; it knows only Rome and not the state in the abstract. The New Testament does not touch a state which is Christian, even in the minimal sense—by which I mean that all its members are Christian. When this happens, has not a change occurred which compels Christians to go beyond the Gospel? Does the simple neutrality of the Gospel suffice for this new situation?

It has been assumed practically since the Act of Milan that the Gospel is not a sufficient guide for life in a Christian state; and one is surprised how easily this has been assumed. Something has been inserted between the kingdom of this world and the eschatological reign which the Bible does not put there. In a matter of such importance one should expect that biblical sources might offer some positive guidance. That they do not may of itself be illuminating; perhaps the Christian should respond to the Christian state as the primitive church responded to Rome. What can be said is that the New Testament foresees no Christian state, and that it has no specific recommendations for behavior in a Christian state.

I pass over the historical question of whether there has ever been a genuine Christian state because it is not relevant; I know that I should have no trouble finding support for the thesis that the Christian state has never existed. We can ask whether the state is an object of redemption—and this is substantially to ask whether the state can become Christian. Perhaps the question cannot be answered; but the implications of the question should not be exaggerated. Cooking, weaving, metallurgy and such activities have no place in the eschatological region; but they belong to "this age," they are a necessary part of the human condition. They become no problem unless men seek them instead of the reign of God and his righteousness—unless cooking, for instance, were regarded as the supreme human fulfillment. Paul once spoke of those whose god is their belly. In a state which practiced the Caesar cult, he could have spoken of those whose god is their state; and the author of the Apocalypse did speak of them.

The question arises because of the evident contrast between political morality and personal morality; and if there is no political morality beyond the ethics of survival, then the question cannot even arise. It is clear that the Christian must in some situations refuse survival; I do not know whether any system of political morality permits this option to the state. It seems clear also that political morality permits men to do in organized groups what Jesus said they should not do as individuals. This distinction was not made by him. The state does not do good to its enemies. It does not turn the other cheek, or walk the additional mile, or give the cloak when the tunic is demanded. It does not deny itself and take up its cross. It is solicitous about food and clothing, and would be unfaithful to its duty if it considered the lilies of the field and trusted in its heavenly Father. It defends itself by arms, apparently excepting itself from the saying of Jesus that they who take the sword perish by the sword. I have already noticed that Paul sees no room for law and courts in a Christian community. The state becomes an impersonal and therefore an amoral entity; but can it ever become really impersonal?

It can be argued, of course, that the state provides for the citizens necessary services and protection which they are unable to secure as individuals; and that therefore its morality cannot be the morality of the individual man. The Christian ideal can and should be practiced by the Christian in his personal relations; it cannot be practiced in his political relations. This position has some validity; but it can be asked to what extent the citizen enjoys the freedom to live the purely personal relations. In how many of his actions is he the political animal and not the Christian free of political obligations? An examination of this problem might disclose that the Christian has very little free room left to live according to Christian charity. The influence of the state is far more extensive than its power, even in what are called free democratic societies. It is magnificent testimonial to the moral integrity of the United States of America that with the exception of Vietnam it has presented to its Christian citizens no moral problem of sufficient magnitude and complexity to warrant a serious theological discussion. One wonders whether such unblemished probity could be found even in the government of the Catholic Church.

If this be thought cynical—and it will be—let us consider the alternative. The alternative is that the actions of the government are not subject to the moral judgment of the individual citizen. Our morality of the state can be reduced to the simple and single obligation of obeying the state, because the state is the supreme judge of what it must do in order to fulfill its duty. And if this be the basic principle of political morality, it becomes easier to understand why the New Testament does not distinguish between a just and an unjust government. No one of us wants to put our own government on what we think is the moral level of Señor Castro's; but both governments are dedicated to their own end, which is survival. If Jesus were asked the question about tribute in Cuba, would his answer be different from what it was in Judaea—or what it would be in the United States? Then and now the citizen must obey the state because only the government has the information on which its decisions are based.

I do not wish to affirm or even to imply that the state has become the supreme arbiter of morality on the political life of the citizen; but I have no hesitation in affirming that it has happened before. Have I any reason to doubt that it can happen in any state? Is there something demonic in the very constitution of the state which drives it ultimately to play God in determining the moral life of its citizens? And will not a Christian state do this perhaps more quickly than a secular state, given the tendency of Christians to be assured that God is on the side of their good conscience? The history of the church united with the Christian state is too largely a history of Caesaropapism.

If the state cannot survive except as a secular amoral entity, one can see why the attitude of the New Testament is neutral. If the state arrogates to itself the right to make supreme moral judgments, it becomes the Beast of the Apocalypse. The New Testament does not recommend rebellion in such cases; it recommends martyrdom and nothing else. The state will endure until God's judgment strikes it; while it endures, the Christian in such a state has no choice except to hold to his loyalty to the reign of God—to which the secular state will transfer him. But even in these exceptional crises, the state remains a part, and a necessary part, of the human condition.

The human condition is the condition of fallen and sinful man. From this condition the state cannot redeem him. It is a part of the human condition as death, concupiscence and nature are a part. Man cannot escape the state; he has to live in a political society. There is no virtue in living in a political society any more than there is virtue in being mortal. It is one of the things which man must endure because he lives under a curse. In the reign of God he will be redeemed from this as from other elements of the curse. His redemption is achieved in and through the human condition, of which the state is a part.

These questions, considerations and doubts may suggest an excessive otherworldliness. They may be taken to imply a flight from social responsibility and the construction of a Christian ghetto neither influencing nor influenced by the political life of man. If they are so taken, the same interpretation could be placed on observations that the state of the Christian is heaven and that the Christian has no enduring city here; and I did not write these observations. One who lives the Christian life described in the Gospels will fairly surely fulfill his social responsibilities. Jesus told his disciples to love their enemies; he did not tell them to be good citizens, but if they love their enemies the recommendation of good citizenship is superfluous.

No, the Christian must live in the state, and he must live in it as a Christian. His Christian life is the only security the state has against becoming the Beast and the Great Whore. As long as a sufficient number of citizens insist that the state remain within its limits, it will do its duty and be less of an obstacle to the establishment of the reign of God. The state which knows that its citizens will refuse it a total commitment will find it difficult to institute modern versions of the Caesar cult. The state whose citizens will not permit it to attempt what it cannot do may more surely accomplish the things it can do. But here we risk building a Utopia. The neutrality of the Gospels is an extremely realistic attitude. If you ask the New Testament what the state can accomplish, the answer is: nothing. Whether it is better or worse, it cannot construct a lasting city. The Christian deals with his state as he deals with his food, his clothing and his house. Like them, it is necessary. Like them, it is used up, it is consumed, it wears out. Like them, it can become a preoccupation which excludes any other interest. The New Testament has no philosophy of the state and no political ethics because Rome, viewed in the light of the Gospels, was essentially trivial.

## Chapter Two

# EVALUATING THE DELUGE MYTH

**C**ONTEMPORARY BIBLICAL studies carried on by Catholic scholars have excited considerable interest within the Catholic community, interest which is both flattering and hostile. Catholic scholars are convinced that they are doing no more than executing the mandate which Pius XII gave them in the encyclical *Divino Afflante Spiritu* of 1943. The scrutiny to which their work has been subjected has disclosed nothing in the biblical movement as a whole which can be defined as a deviation from the mandate.

Popular interest in biblical studies has usually been centered on the *conclusions* of the scholars rather than on their methods, for the good reason that acquaintance with the methods of biblical studies can be gained only by prolonged and assiduous application to these studies. But of late, interest has more and more turned to the methods; Catholics would like to have a clearer idea of how scholars arrive at their conclusions. This article is intended to be a sample of methods as applied to a question now regarded as closed in modern interpretation: the story of the deluge. Because it is closed, no doubts should arise about the use of the methods here. And where the methods have been proved valid, it is legitimate to extend them to other problems which admit the same type of analysis. Obviously it cannot be

23

determined whether these other problems admit the same analysis until the analysis is attempted.

That the deluge, related in Genesis 6-9, was a historical event narrated exactly as it happened was not questioned until the nineteenth century. To say that it could not have been questioned may be too much. We can now see how the question could have been raised; this does not imply that earlier scholars ought to have raised it. The acceptance of the spherical shape of the earth and the knowledge of its vast dimensions led some interpreters to question whether the deluge was properly universal; but with this reservation the historical character of the account was not otherwise seriously doubted.

What reasons now appear for raising the question? One is the obvious assumption that the story of the deluge, like the other elements of Genesis 1-11, presents a condition of man altogether different from the known conditions of historic man. In other collections of folklore the creation of an imaginary world so different from the world of experience is clear evidence that we deal with something other than history. But it was assumed without question that biblical narrative never deals with things other than history, that fiction of any kind is beneath the dignity of God and of the Bible, the word of God. If this faith in biblical history compelled one to assume the existence of an unrealistic world, then the assumption was accepted. Biblical discourse moved in the biblical universe, and both were subject to their own laws. One left the world of experience when one entered the world of the Bible. In the world of the Bible anything could happen.

Very few protests against this position were heard before the nineteenth century; and those who did protest hurt their position by the manner and tone of their protests. Like the orthodox, they thought that fictitious narrative was unworthy of the Bible; and they uttered their doubts as a part of a denial of the historical and religious value of the Bible. They were incapable of attaching any value other than the historical to the deluge story. Consequently, their protests were rightly stigmatized as "rationalism," and the Christian churches, both Catholic and Protestant, refused to take account of the protests. It was still too early to consider the deluge story for its theological significance.

What turned the direction of interpretation was the discovery of the Mesopotamian deluge story. This story is found in the XI tablet of the Epic of Gilgamesh, discovered in the vast library collected at Nineveh by Ashurbanipal, king of Assyria, 668-630 B.C. Other fragments of the epic show that the Akkadian form of the poem is at least as old as the Old Babylonian period, the first part of the second millennium B.C. In 1914, a fragment of the Sumerian form of the poem which shows that the poem existed in the third millennium B.C. was published. In the Akkadian form, the hero of the poem, Gilgamesh, journeys to the ends of the earth in search of the plant of life, and there he encounters Ut-napishtim, who with his wife has survived the deluge and is granted immortality by the gods. The story as told in answer to the request of Gilgamesh relates that Enlil became angry with man and was determined to destroy him; but Ut-napishtim was forewarned by the god Ea, who favored him. At Ea's instructions he built a huge boat with seven decks, into which he took his family and animals and craftsmen, lest the crafts perish. After a rain of a week's duration which brought total inundation, the boat finally came to rest on a mountain. Ut-napishtim sent out a dove, a swallow and a raven to find whether the waters had run off. He then came forth and offered sacrifice, at which the gods assembled. When Enlil found that Ut-napishtim had escaped, he was angered. But Ea charged him with excess; he should have sent a lesser agent of his anger such as a wild beast, famine or pestilence.

It was evident when the Gilgamesh epic was deciphered and translated, that the epic and Genesis 6-9 related the same story. It was equally evident that the Mesopotamian deluge story was of earlier origin than the Genesis account; in any hypothesis of Israelite origins, the deluge story was written long before any group called Israel came into existence. If there is any literary dependence, it is dependence of Israel on Mesopotamia. And literary dependence there must be; if it does not exist here, it exists nowhere. The dependence is shown by much more than the common account of a deluge in which one family escapes by the construction of a barge. It appears in little details like the animals of the ark and the use of the birds to ascertain whether the deluge has abated. The differences are no more than one expects to find when a folklore story passes into another language and another culture. The Israelite knew nothing about the building of boats, and the story does not have a boat; it has an "ark," a floating box or house modeled on the craft of Ut-napishtim. The hero was Ziusudra in Sumerian, Ut-napishtim in Akkadian, and Noah in Hebrew. It is no more necessary to explain how he became Noah than it is to explain how he became Ut-napishtim. Finally the geography of the Genesis story is Mesopotamian, not Palestinian.

Naturally, the thought occurs that the deluge story is an account of a historical event preserved in Mesopotamia and in Israel. The trouble with this suggestion is that the Mesopotamian deluge is obviously not the story of a historical event; it is mythological. The Israelite story contains no element which is surely independent of the Mesopotamian story; the difference lies in the theology of the story, not in the details of the account. The suggestion that Genesis preserves the memory of a historical event through the medium of a Mesopotamian myth is so evidently contrived that it falls of its own weight. That floods occurred in Mesopotamia is obvious, but it is not to the point; the flood in the myth is cosmic not Mesopotamian.

But the Israelite writers have not preserved the Mesopotamian deluge story. They have rewritten it substantially so that it communicates an altogether different idea. In both forms of the story the actions of divine beings and the relations between the divine and the human are not accessory; they are essential to the narrative. It is not merely a story of a deluge, but rather an encounter of man with the divine. Each story is a revelation of the divine; but that which is revealed about the divine is dissimilar. The Israelite story is dependent on the Mesopotamian story; but the divine being in the Israelite story is not dependent on the Mesopotamian story. The divine being is the God of Israelite revelation, and his actions in the story are characteristic of him as he is known throughout the Old Testament. This is the specifically Israelite element in the story; and the introduction of the Israelite God has transformed the story.

An enumeration of the antitheses between the two stories in this respect will make clear what the Israelite authors accomplished. The Mesopotamian story is initiated by the decision of Enlil to destroy mankind. This decision is unmotivated. The biblical story places the motive in the wickedness of man, and the deluge becomes not an act of capricious anger but an act of judgment. In the Mesopotamian story the hero of the deluge is saved by the secret revelation of Ea, another god. Within the monotheism of the Bible no such divergence of purpose is possible; Noah is spared through the revelation of the same God who brings the flood, and he is saved because he is innocent of the wickedness which elicits the judgment. The Israelite God intends to renew mankind, not to destroy it. After the deluge there can be no dispute among the gods in the Israelite story. Where Ea charges Enlil with excessive anger, Yahweh makes a covenant by which he pledges himself that there will not be another totally destructive deluge. Noah is not rewarded with immortality, for Israelite thought knew nothing of human beings who were granted this prerogative.

Behind these differences lie divergent complexes of ideas. Neither the Mesopotamian nor the Israelite deluge story are clear by themselves; each story illuminates the other and shows what the authors intended to do. By comparison it becomes clear that to call these "flood stories" is to miss the major theme. The stories are concerned with a much deeper problem than the flood itself; and against this problem, discussion of the historical character of the flood or of its extension can look trivial. In the ancient world the myth explored and stated problems which in the recent and modern world are discussed in philosophy and theology. The problem touched on in the Mesopotamian myth is the nature of the gods and their attitude toward mankind exhibited in the phenomena of nature. An answer to the problem is given in the myth.

The cosmic deluge is an example of the destructive forces of nature. The dimensions of the catastrophe exceed any known historical incident, but the principle does not depend on the number of persons involved. The problem is simply that men often die by the concurrence of natural forces, and sometimes in numbers so large that they are shocking. The Sumerians and the Babylonians did not treat this problem as one of nature; nature was the field of divine activity, all natural occurrences were the effect of the will of the gods. To the question why the gods should will the destruction of men, the deluge story shows that there is no answer. When the gods are angry, men perish; but man should not look for a rational motivation of the divine anger. The anger of the gods may be rational or it may be capricious; it makes no difference to man whether it is one or the other, for man is equally helpless in either case.

When Ea protests against the excess of Enlil, he speaks for Mesopotamian man. The Mesopotamian accepted the irrational caprice of the gods; it was a personal interpretation of phenomena which are irrational viewed personally. He had learned to live with the gods, for the same will which brought death conferred life. His happiness lay in adjusting himself to this will in all its unpredictability. But there were limits beyond which the Mesopotamian felt the gods should not go. Such were the massive disasters which sweep away human life as if it were so much rubbish. He could tolerate lesser agents such as predatory beasts, famine and disease, but when the whole of nature turned against him, he felt that the gods had passed the limits of decent anger. Does this protest have its roots in the memory of some prehistoric disaster? No doubt it does, but one need not think that the disaster was the deluge described in the story. The protest arises from man's experience of nature as hostile, and his identification of this hostility with the anger of the gods.

To the Israelite such a conception of God and nature was intolerable. The Israelites, too, experienced God in nature, and interpreted its phenomena as the effects of his will. Their idea of nature and natural forces was no more impersonal than the Mesopotamians. When nature afflicted them, they took it as an act of the anger of God. They could not attribute to the God whom they worshipped a capricious and irrational anger. If God were angry, his anger was rationally motivated and explicable.

If he were angry at men, it was because men gave him cause for anger; and men do this by rebellion. Nature is the arm of God's punishment of the wicked; and in most of the Old Testament this principle is followed rigorously to its conclusion. Those who are punished are wicked; the wrath of God exhibited in nature is sufficient evidence for us. If Sodom and Gomorrah are totally destroyed, it is because there is no single righteous person left after Lot and his family were led forth. An obvious corollary to this subject is the universal sickness of mankind; and this corollary the Israelites accepted.

Yet they accepted it with reservations. The idea of a God who was consumed with anger was foreign to Israelite belief. If God were angry, it was righteous anger; but righteous anger had to be tempered with mercy if it were to remain righteous. Man is wicked, but he is also weak in confrontation with God; and God takes account of his weakness. In the biblical deluge story the convenant in which God pledges not to annihilate man entirely corresponds to the speech of Ea in the Mesopotamian story. The biblical account is not a rebuke of God, as Ea rebukes Enlil; but it affirms that such total wrath is not suitable to God. God punished man in moderation, less than man deserves. Having punished totally once, he will not do it again.

This may seem to be a quite primitive theological view, and so it is; but we must consider the theological view to which it was opposed. The Israelite encountered in the Mesopotamian deluge story a theory of nature and the gods proposed with some imagination and vigor. The theory was congenial to Mesopotamian religion and gave man a certain satisfaction in his despair. He simply renounced any effort to find moral patterns in the behavior of the gods; and he was thus released from the compulsion to find moral patterns in his own life. The Israelite found this view expressed in myth. He did not compose a theoretical refutation; he rewrote the myth. The God who acts in the deluge story is the same God who acts throughout the Old Testament. The Israelite inserted him into the deluge story and thus showed that the Mesopotamian view was not imposed even in the thought patterns of the deluge myth. A story which originally was a statement of divine unrighteousness becomes in Israelite hands a story of divine righteousness and a vindication of the divine will that men should be righteous.

I present this as a sample of modern methods of interpretation. The first question which the interpreter asks is not, "What happened?" but, "What does this text mean?" In this instance the Mesopotamian sources of the deluge story show us the patterns of thought and the forms of literature in which the biblical writer moves. They show us the thesis his own story opposes. He employs the same techniques of imagination and narrative which the Mesopotamian writers employed; he meets them on their own ground in order to arrive at an idea of God different from theirs. He shows literary dependence on the Mesopotamian writings; but he shows theological independence. The God of whom he writes is not a God of his own invention, but the God who revealed himself in Israel. The deluge story so understood makes sense in its own literary type, which is the myth; we can see what the author intended to do and the means which he used to accomplish his purpose.

*Chapter Three*

# CRIME AND PUNISHMENT

FOR SOME TIME the thought has been recurring that I ought to attempt a theological discussion of crime and punishment. The thought recurs with greater urgency now that two highbrow journals which I read regularly, *The Center Magazine* and *The American Scholar,* have recently published symposia on this topic. The contributors were mostly attorneys and professors of law, police officers and civic administrators, and a dash of sociologists and political theorists. It did not occur to the editors to invite theologians to contribute; I shall shortly set forth my own reasons why I do not think that theologians have anything to say. *The Center* symposium was marred, in my judgment, by the contributions of some radical lawyers who do not seem to have grasped very well what law is. *The American Scholar* symposium was remarkable for the broad spectrum of competent opinion it presented and for the tone of the writing, which was objective without losing compassion. Neither symposium attempted to solve the problem and they ought to silence those who offer facile solutions. There is a certain hard core of insolubility in the problem of crime, for which a theological designation would be concupiscence. But no one thinks that crime has to be as far out of control as it seems to be.

The reason why theologians seem to have nothing to say is that European Christianity, whether Catholic or Protestant, has lent its religious sanction to a penal system which endured for centuries and is now thought barbarous. A novelist—I think the

31

costume writer Thomas B. Costain—describes some early Spanish explorers sailing into a West Indian harbor and sighting on the shore gibbets from which natives were suspended. One officer remarks to another, "Thank God, we are back in a Christian country." Nasty, but not entirely distorted. The moral principles by which Christian theologians dealt with crime and punishment were the ethical principles of the just war. They are as bankrupt in one case as they are in the other.

It does come to mind, however, that this is neither the place nor the writer for this question. At best it is theological journalism by a writer whose specialization has not been in Christian moral theology. Hence my purpose is to modestly raise a few questions which my colleagues, I hope, will pursue further with their own proper skill. Raising "questions" may take the form of gratuitous assertions, but my colleagues will know how to deal with this.

I would first like to remind discussants that law and justice are not synonymous and coterminous. This was known and uttered by the Israelite prophets. Modern students of the humanities are more likely to be introduced to "the higher law" of the *Antigone* and the *Crito* that the citizen cannot obey unjust laws, but that he must take the legal consequences of his refusal. Law at best is an attempt to get some justice for some people. It is also at its best when it expresses a popular consensus, as our law theoretically does. But one can have complete observance of the law without achieving justice. Law is subject to constant change to meet the demands of justice, and a system of courts is instituted to protect the individual citizen from the injustice so often implicit in law. With all these reservations, the human experience so far is that law, however imperfect it is, is a better assurance of justice than anarchy is.

I would next like to see some nonsense removed from the discussion of crime and punishment. The nonsense I have in mind is this. We have inherited a penal system thousands of years old. We may have certain purposes in mind, but the nature of the penal system is substantially determined by history. Philosophers speak of the end of the act—its objective purpose—as distinct from the end of the agent—its subjective purpose. The objective purpose of the penal system has always been to punish the offender; and if one polishes up one's Latin one will notice that "punish" means to inflict pain. The old ethical name for this act of justice, as it has been called so long, is vindictive justice; you have pained us, now we are going to pain you. During most of human history the pain was death or mutilation; our ancestors saw no reason for spending money on criminals, and incarceration is a modern penalty. The objective purpose of the penalty had nothing to do with deterrence; the only person who was deterred from the crime was the person punished. Others may profit by his example, but if they did not this was no reason to dispense from punishment. Neither was society protecting itself by execution, at least directly. It is still argued whether punishment in any degree is such a protection, although experience seems to assure that swift sure punishment deters some and affords more protection than uncertain punishment. Again, the only person against whom society protects itself in this process is the criminal. It does not stop "crime." And nothing was further from the purpose of the traditional penal system than correction or rehabilitation.

I imply no value judgment hereby. Crime properly defined—and hardly anyone would deny that this includes crime against the person—is a form of barbarism. Traditionally it was punished with barbarism. There ought to be a better way. But as long as we maintain the forms of legal penology, we ought to be aware of what they mean.

I must also advert to certain defects in the operation of the legal system which permit some to say that the system ought to be abolished. If I speak of Chicago and Illinois, it is because the Chicago newspapers are the only newspapers I read regularly; other communities have their own problems with public servants, I suppose. Everyone who owns or drives a car must deal with the Secretary of State, and the very ownership and operation places one in contact with the law. Law as a work of justice is not promoted by the discovery that the last Secretary of State left $850,000 in cash at his death. I wish I could remember the name of the Chicago journalist who said that this shows what can be accomplished by thrift, careful management and prudent investment. Law is not promoted when we learn that our legislators and administrators use their public office to invest in opportunities which are not available to others. Law is not promoted when a chief prosecutor sends a party of armed police into an apartment and, it is charged, the police blast two men dead without even challenging them. It will not be promoted, as many of us fear, if the affair is settled by a tap on the wrist. Yet it cannot be reasonably argued that because some legislators and officers of the law do not observe it, or that the cure for corruption is to corrupt everyone.

It is impossible to treat this problem without becoming racist, so here I go. I am told that 75% of recorded crimes in Chicago are committed by blacks, and that 85% of the victims of recorded crimes are black. As someone has said, those who are most concerned with crime in the streets seem to be least threatened by it. One of the contributors to *The American Scholar* symposium, himself a black man from Philadelphia, gives even more appalling statistics for Philadelphia. Rational discourse about this problem seems so impossible that one is tempted to renounce it. We hear that these black criminals are victims of society; that a black man cannot get a fair trial in a white man's court; that black gangsterism is the only expression of manhood allowed a poor young black; that crime is black rage against an imperialist racist social system. And I have not cited all the pleas that are raised to the effect that whenever a black young man is arrested for murder, armed robbery, assault, rape and child molesting, someone else is to blame. We did not talk that way about Jesse James, Al Capone and John Dillinger, who were not charged with political offenses.

I think it should be noticed that the enormous majority of the inhabitants of the ghetto do not commit crimes, and this has to be remembered whenever the ghetto is alleged as the breeding ground of criminals. This is not to say that the ghetto itself is not a crime which cries to heaven for vengeance. Indeed it is; but in our imperialist racist system it is not against the law, and slums never have been against the law. Law is not justice, I have said. Whatever must be done about the ghetto, I see no positive contribution in dashing out the brains of some poor black man for $15, nor in dealing with those who do such things as social protestors and political activists. The ghetto must be destroyed not to wipe out crime, but because it is the only decent thing to do. But while we are destroying the ghetto, which will take more than a month, what can we do to keep black rage from expressing its discontent with the racist system by using bicycle chains on other blacks?

There are other ways of expressing black manhood than gangsterism. Black youths whose bodies are found in alleys with bullets in the head because they refused to join gangs found another way of expressing their manhood. The gangs allow only one such expression to any individual. Angela Davis sees in blacks who succeed in the white man's world the real renegades. I suppose someone has to stick up for losers, but I doubt that they should be armed. I doubt also that they are really rebelling against an unjust system, unless a system is just only when it punishes success and rewards failure. I have read of black radicals who nearly foam at the mouth at the mention of Thurgood Marshall. He committed the supreme treason of working his way to success instead of getting out there with the bicycle chains.

One is a little weary of complaints about the denial of justice to blacks in the white man's courts. I have to point out that if the chief prosecutor is called to account it will be in a white man's court, and the major effort at this writing is to see that he never gets into that court. This is probably significant. I observe that if some black militants had fared as well in the white man's court as Nathan Leopold and Richard Loeb, we would hear of neither again for the rest of their lives. That justice has often been denied the black man is obvious—justice here meaning the kind of justice which one may hope for from the law. If black criminals were judged by their victims in the ghetto they would, I believe, run to the white man's court rather rapidly; although some Chicago gangs have achieved something not known here

since Capone: sudden lapses of memory and failures in vision
in witnesses. These failures can hardly be blamed on the white
man's court. The ghetto may be in a limited way a breeding
ground of crime, but it should be noticed that self-pity helps to
breed crime too.

Finally, we have what many think is the fundamental moral
breakdown, the war in Vietnam, which, some say, is a national
crime against which crime in the streets pales. A nation which
commands, tolerates, forgives or whatever we did to actions like
those of Lieutenant Calley complains about crime in the streets
from a feeble moral posture. The answer seems to be to close up
the moral gap, not to make My Lai the standard of behavior of
American citizens toward each other. Yet, as a student of the
Israelite prophets, I sometimes have fears that in Vietnam we
may, like the ancient Israelites, have passed the point at which
God will not exact the full measure of our collective guilt. And
this means that I am not clear in my mind that we have so much
crime in the nation because it could not happen to a more de-
serving people.

At this point I become more theological in my reflections, and
I realize that I will lose the sociologists, the penologists and the
politicians. I also realize that I have said nothing which could
be construed as a Christian response to crime and punishment.
I know a woman who is the only authentic pacifist of whom I
am sure. Of crime she says simply that she will not resist, that
she would meet the criminal as one in dire need, that she would
give him what he demanded because he is in dire need. I remarked above that our ethics of crime and punishment are our
ethics of the just war. In both questions the existing ethical
forms must be shattered; to coin a phrase, you cannot put new
wine in old skins. My friend has shattered them. She believes
that Jesus has made the only pertinent remark to the question,
that we must forgive, that we must bear iniquity, that we must
go the second mile, and give the cloak in addition to the shirt,
and turn the other cheek. I hope she is not found dying on the
sidewalk some day; but if she should be, she would regard this
as a redemptive work. The criminal, like the law-abiding citizen,

will be saved only by love. He has to be taught the meaning of love by experiencing it. Like enforcement and punishment, it must be done not because it stops crime but because it touches the real individual person. Jesus did not give this a social structure or tell the disciples that they had to do it as soon as everyone else had done it first. If we wait for a socially structured love which it is safe to practice, Lake Michigan will freeze solid first. I suppose I cannot impose this on anyone; it is the mission of the church to proclaim the gospel. But as a theologian I can say that I have seen no other response to crime and punishment which can claim to be Christian. Other responses proceed as if the Incarnation had never happened. Add to the system of crime and punishment such ornaments as deterrence and rehabilitation, and it is substantially the same system which we find in the code of Hammurabi. It does not effectively seek reconciliation. Unless my colleagues can create some significant thinking in this direction, I might as well reread Hammurabi. As a recent fugitive from surgery, I have secretly been enjoying his law which prescribes that the surgeon who injures his patient shall have his right hand severed.

*Chapter Four*

# AND THE TWO . . .
# REMAIN TWO

I HAVE THOUGHT a long time that popes, cardinals, bishops, priests (including monsignori, pastors and theologians) and laymen like Joe Breig and Dale Francis talk entirely too much about sex and too little about other things like justice, mercy and faith.

However, the topic of sex took form in my mind when I read a single issue of the *Chicago Daily News;* this is a tribute to the stimulating qualities of this generally excellent newspaper. I first read Mike Royko, one of the sages of the *Daily News.* I need not summarize the whole column; what impressed me was his sane treatment of pornographic movies, which can be summarized in one sentence: "(People) don't really care to see clean movies themselves, but it bothers them that somebody else is seeing dirty ones." Then on the editorial page Sydney Harris, another sage of the *Daily News,* says of sexual permissiveness: "The tragedy is that the young people no longer care whether I . . . or millions like us, approve or disapprove. We have lost their attention, and right or wrong, they are going to make their own mistakes, and not copy ours. It is hard to blame them." Harris believes that sexual permissiveness is just part of vast and deep social changes, and that one cannot talk sense about it apart from the whole social scene. So much from two of the best journalistic commentators in the United States. Neither is ever shallow. They may not like to hear this, but they are both powerful moral voices in this community, and I am glad that they are.

I read these two pieces with substantial agreement. I suggested above that I hear too much from the clergy about sex. Let me add now that what I hear is mostly moral imperialism, the imposition of decisions made by men who, if they are what they claim to be, can have no more than book knowledge about the subject. It has long been my conviction that here we can proclaim nothing except personal responsibility and freedom of decision. Much Catholic preaching about sex is incredible, impractical and Gnostic, and this includes more than birth control.

Then I passed through the women's page and read an anonymous piece which received that day's award for amateur journalism. The writer was a woman eighteen years of age. Since the boy is called John, let us call her Mary; these are the standard names both in cases in moral theology and in stories which used to be told in Pullman washrooms (what has replaced the Pullman washroom as this masculine situation in life?). Mary has just had an abortion. She and John have been sleeping together for three years (I make that since she was fifteen, if she can count, of which I am not sure). This information raises other questions about their relationship which it would be indelicate to pursue. In the crisis John was simply great. He bought not one but two tickets to New York, told her parents they were going to a state park for a picnic, flew to New York with her, and held her hand all the way back to Chicago. It was all done in one day. She wishes that she were not so isolated from her family, but believes that they would not understand her. I think what she means is that she is afraid they will understand her. She feels much closer to John, and since she is going on the Pill she is free from fear. The experience included among its other rewarding features the fact that for the first time in her life no one seemed to be passing judgment on her. And she closes by telling us, not without pathos, that nothing has changed; John just called up and wants her to go out for pizza. Pizza?

I read this and went into the bathroom and tried to throw up. It seemed to be the only proper response. Then the horrible thought occurred that I had been had by the *Daily News,* or that both the Daily News and I had been had by some imaginative writer. I would prefer to think this, and to praise the writer for creating one of the most nauseating females in literature since Milady de Winter. This kid, real or fictitious, makes Clytemnestra look like Elsie Dinsmore. John and Mary, the little dears, are thoroughly vicious. They make me a little happier that more of my life has been used than remains to be used; and this means that their sickness is communicating itself to me. Togetherness through abortion—it would make a title for a soap opera: John and Mary, holding hands through life and death— the deaths of other people—and sharing the wonder of their love over a pizza. I wonder if I can ever eat a pizza again without recurring nausea at the thought of this pair.

But what is so bad about an abortion, or about concubinage? Both are too common to excite horror, and my own reaction is a puzzle to me. I am uncertain about abortion; I have a gut feeling that it is wrong, but those who defend it have a gut feeling that it is right. Moral problems should not be solved by gut feelings. I can no longer accept the total prohibition of Catholic morality; some questions cannot be resolved by this prohibition except by treating the person as a thing. A mother has a sure right to life as a person which is not as well established as a fetus; on the other hand, how free are we to treat the fetus as garbage?

Similarly, I believe traditional Catholic morality has taken an entirely legalistic view of marriage. We have identified marriage with the ceremony, the only thing which can be juridically established. This is surely the symbol of the reality rather than the reality. Again, the prohibition of divorce on the basis of a ceremony and the prohibition of carnal commerce without the ceremony seems to treat persons as things. On the other hand, the sexual union of man and woman does have social implications. In spite of these doubts, John and Mary nauseate me. A few years ago I had an interesting discussion about extramarital sex with an intelligent and educated young Catholic wife, really a rather sweet girl. She insisted, quite properly, that two people must find "a meaningful interpersonal relationship." Desirous of a broader moral context of discussion, and somewhat offended by statements that I lack understanding, I said, rather rudely, I fear: "I understand quite well what you mean. It is just that what you call a meaningful interpersonal relationship we old fogies have been accustomed to call casual fornication." I was wrong. It is fornication, but in the best circles it is not casual. It is unfair to our younger contemporaries to think that the Manson family are their heroes.

If John and Mary have achieved a meaningful interpersonal relationship, then I should withdraw from society and become a hermit. What offended me was not concubinage and abortion so much as the completely candid and utterly shallow amorality of Mary's prize essay. She—and since she and John are closer than ever now, I assume it goes for him too—manifests a dedicated selfishness which would be infantile in a child of five. She hurts all the time because she feels people are passing judgment on her. Well, no wonder; and since she turned her piece in to the newspaper, I take it she makes it a matter of public discussion. If her family has not been passing judgment on her, they suffer from acne of the conscience as much as she does. Is she possibly a victim of society, a product of upper middle class suburbia?

I am offended also because I see these morally retarded children playing with life. It is not safe in their hands. And there is another unpleasantness hidden in their attitude and in the response of many adults to such affairs. The fumbling adolescent exploration of sex has been going on since Eve gave birth to the unnamed sisters of Cain and Abel. It has always been known and always been tolerated by the elders as a necessary evil in the process of growing up. Nobody has ever said it is good. This is the first time in the history of our culture, as far as I know, that anyone has tried to rationalize it, has seriously proposed that adolescent sex fumbling is an authentic way of life, and that it is a more honest attitude toward sex than the way of marriage. John and Mary have nothing to teach their elders about sexual morality; and when that state park story is considered, they have nothing to teach their elders about hypocrisy.

Mary has given us an unusually good insight into adolescent depravity; I find it no more attractive than adult depravity. My experience of her age group does not permit me to think she is typical.

I confess to an old-fashioned reverence for sex, and it revolts me to see anyone, adolescent or adult, playing house as if it were tennis. The sexual relation of man and woman is the most intimate personal exchange known to man, and it was a biblical author who said that the two become one. We say this of no other meaningful interpersonal relationship. If the person is sacred, surely that sacredness is nowhere more manifest than in sexual union. It is not just reverence for sex which I feel, it is reverence for the person. There is a unique personal commitment in sexual union, a baring of the inner self of which the baring of the body is a mere symbol, a surrender to helpless dependence on another. To reduce this to the shallow and the trivial seems to be a profanation of the sacredness of the person, a degradation of the self at the moment of its greatest potentiality for fullness. This also, I submit, is treating persons as things.

And now, Mike Royko, I do not believe I am worrying about what is in the next person's shopping bag. I did not ask Mary to lay out the contents of her own shopping bag in the *Daily News,* nor did I give her a bond for the revelation. If the world knows her story it is because she told it in a newspaper which is read by several hundred thousand people. If she has the freedom to relate her story and win a prize (which will help, I am sure, to pay for that trip to New York and those pizzas and the Pill), I think I have the freedom to say that her story is incomprehensible to me. I said I am in substantial agreement with your position; I will add to your position that one way to keep me from criticizing what is in another's shopping bag is not to spread its contents before me. I might just puke.

As for you, Sydney Harris, are you still ready to accept the fact that they will make their own mistakes, not ours? I suppose that this is the ultimate freedom, the freedom to make one's own mistakes. There is also the freedom to say that it is a mistake.

Would you like to try to convince John and Mary that they have made their own mistake? Dear me no, they made no mistake; they did exactly right; whatever they want to do is right. We wrongly assume that they are making a mistake. They are actually revealing to us a new and honest morality of interpersonal relationship, Sydney. It depresses me. If I were not a celibate, I would call up my girl friend and invite her out for a pizza.

Must I end this on a note of bitterness and cynicism? Is there no hope that John and Mary will some day, some how, learn to help make a decent world? It sounds as if Mary has never experienced love, or did not recognize it; she is without it because she does not know how. She has identified love with the experience of sex, the reality with the symbol. She is unaware of the larger dimensions of love, and there is no book for this. Who is to tell her to repent and believe the gospel when she knows nothing of which she should repent? Who is to tell her to go and sin no more when she does not know she has sinned at all? She will never learn the dimensions of love until she has experienced the total gift of self; and until some one appears who makes her this gift, the church, I fear, has nothing to say to which she is likely to listen. She and John will continue to seek togetherness through the sharing of bed, pizza and abortion.

Chapter Five

# ROOM FOR THE SACRED

A NUMBER of my colleagues in the publishing field have recently commented upon the Vatican document issuing directives for the garb of religious women. Their interpretation of the document rests on an assumed principle that the Holy See sometimes closes a question by a declaration so outrageous that no one can think they mean it seriously. A few years ago, I myself urged that this—I used more discreet language—was the principle by which the encyclical on birth control should have been interpreted; and that it was only the refusal of some to be satisfied with decent interment of the question that compelled the Holy See to advance to positions which it had never expected to defend. By coincidence, I had a recent conversation about these new directives with some religious women, who noticed, once they had read the document, that it prohibited nothing which had been done in their own communities. This suggests that the document was a more successful use of obscure language than *Human Vitae* in that under a great deal of conservative sound and fury it really said nothing. But neither the language nor the style of pontifical government is my interest here, and still less, religious garb; I expressed myself on this topic a few years ago. I am interested in the sacred.

Now the "sacred" is found in every religion; the interested reader can pursue it in many books, among which I recommend the classic writings of G. van der Leeuw and Mircea Eliade. The sacred is the area of contact between man and the divinity, and this area is chosen by the deity himself; it is not for man to lay down terms according to which he will deal with the deity. The sacred is an area of space, an interval of time, a class of persons, and the apparatus of liturgical worship; these are normal in religion. Their sacredness rests on the divine choice of the place, the time, the persons and the tools of worship through which he is pleased to be approached by men. Historians of religion find some other explanation than authentic divine choice for the sacred; as one writer said in another connection, and I paraphrase his words, the reason why Zeus cannot choose sacred times and places and persons is that Zeus does not exist and never did. Now granting the belief which I share with my fellow Christians that Yahweh of Israel and the Father of Jesus designate one and the same real divine being, does it follow from his reality that certain sacred items in Israel, judaism and Christianity derive their sacredness from an equally real divine election? The one reality does not logically compel the affirmation of the other. A religion which worships a real deity may have a sacred place which is no more really associated with that deity than the Parthenon was with Athene.

The sacred was known in Israel and Judaism. Early Israel had a number of sacred places by which they understood that the deity could be worshiped there; it is very probable that these places were recognized as sacred by the cultic legend of a theophany. Israel had sacred times, the festivals at which Yahweh had declared that he met his people in worship. Israel had its sacred personnel, obscure in its origins and history, but issuing in the Aaronic priesthood which served in what became the only sacred place of Judaism, the temple of Jerusalem. This spot is still a sacred place, but it is now sacred in Islam.

Greek and Roman religions, which the first Christians knew, also had sacred places, times and persons. We could not even begin to enumerate them; again, the interested reader can pursue the topic in the standard work of Nilsson, which describes the religious world in which the church first appeared. Greek and Roman religions, like Israelite religion and Judaism, are thoroughly typical in the manifestation and use of the sacred.

No value judgment about the sacred is implied. Clearly it serves as a sensible symbol of the presence and action of the deity, and as such it is indifferent whether the deity symbolized is "true" or not. The symbol will serve a true god or a false god equally well.

It seems to me that we do not sufficiently attend to the degree to which primitive apostolic Christianity, the Christianity of the New Testament, departs from the pattern of the sacred both in Judaism and in Hellenistic religion. The Greek word for "priest" is used of no church officer in the New Testament, and it is dishonest to say that the New Testament has the equivalent. The priest was a known cultic officer of a distinct character; the apostolic church did not use this word because it had no cultic office to which to apply it. The church in its origins had no sacred personnel, and this was emphasized by Paul, who affirms more than once that he did not sustain himself by his ministry. He was a tentmaker, and in modern terms he was a full-time tentmaker and a part-time apostle. This may come from rabbinical influence; the rabbis believed that a man should not support himself by his teaching, but should earn his living otherwise and teach for free. Evidently neither the modern churchman nor the modern educator is able to live by the rabbinical principle, nor is the modern rabbi. According to Paul neither did all the apostles. They may indeed have been professional religious persons in the sociological sense, persons whose only employment is religion; sacred persons they were not, neither in the Jewish, Greek nor modern sense.

The absence of sacred personnel begins to look like part of a pattern when we see that the apostolic church had no sacred places. They met for worship in a house or a hired hall. They cherished no memory of the places where Jesus had lived and died—even of the place where he had risen. They knew what temples were, and they did not have them. The first properties Christian communities owned, and this was later than the New Testament, were cemeteries; burial societies were a common form of legal free association under Roman law, and most "churches" existed officially as burial societies. Oddly enough, the cemeteries were the first places to become sacred. Paul recognized no Christian temple except the body of the individual believer (I Corinthians 6:19); wherever the Christian is, there is a sacred place. Paul was a Jew and knew the temple; he is said in Acts to have worshiped there after his conversion. When Paul had no temple in the Christian church he knew what he was implying. Of sacred times we may say simply that we know of no sacred days or seasons in the apostolic church. The churches met for worship on Sundays; since this was just another day in the Roman week, it could not be regarded as sacred.

These considerations go far beyond the question of religious garb with which I began. What we see in the apostolic church is an abandonment of the ancient and accepted category of the sacred. The sacred means, we have noticed, the designated times, places and personnel through which God is experienced. In the apostolic church God was experienced more directly and immediately. We can find words in the New Testament to designate this direct and immediate experience. No one would question that the primary word to designate the experience of God is love; God is encountered in the loving communion of the members of the church with each other. This is not an experience, if I may be forgiven the expression, for which hierarchical directives are necessary. God is experienced in the indwelling Spirit who is given to all believers in the sacraments of initiation and who manifests himself in the charismatic works which he empowers all the members of the church to perform. These charismatic works are not the works exclusively of sacred personnel. As far as sacred places and times are concerned, God is equally available at any time and place. As far as sacred personnel are concerned, every believer becomes a member of the sacred personnel.

One may conjecture that a religion in which the sacred is abolished is a religion apt to transcend political and social divisions. One may ask whether Paul, who said that in Christ there is neither Jew nor Greek, slave nor free, male nor female (Galatians 3:28), should have added, if he had thought of it, that there are in Christ, clergy and laity, religious and secular, and to that extent you are not all one in Christ Jesus. One notices that the writer of I Peter (who for conservative theologians has to be Peter) describes the church as a chosen race, a royal priesthood, a holy nation, God's own people (2:9). Surely clergy and religious are a little more chosen, a little more royal, a little more holy, a little more God's own people? Early Christians may have thought, as we do not, that Jesus had initiated the new convenant of Jeremiah (31:31-34), in which each man shall no longer teach his neighbor and teach his brother, saying "Know the Lord"; for they shall all know the Lord, from the least of them to the greatest. To paraphrase this in the jargon of theology, they may have thought that the revelation of God in Jesus Christ brought God closer to the individual person than he had been in Israel, and that Jeremiah meant it when he said that in the future no system of priests and teachers like the Israelite system would be required.

The Catholic Church did not get its sacred places and its sacred personnel from the New Testament. It got them from the religious symbolism of Judaism and Hellenistic-Roman paganism. Our churches and the liturgical pageantry carried on inside them continue the ritual of the Jerusalem temple and the Roman temples. I remember being offended at the inscriptions so common on baroque churches in Rome commemorating the Roman nobles who donated the building with hardly a mention of the deity or his friends. I am no longer offended by what is right and proper. Those buildings are what their builders intended them to be, monuments to the Farnese and the like and not to God. The Roman Pontiff, *romanus pontifex,* was a cultic officer of the Roman Republic, continued in the Empire and surviving only in the Roman Catholic Church; and it would be petulant to suggest that the church might have gone to some other source than Roman paganism for this official designation.

It comes down to the question whether we believe that Jesus established a viable church—a perfect society, as the theologians call it, one which has within itself all the resources to fulfill its purpose. The question is whether the apostolic church rejected the sacred on principle or because it was too poor to afford it; whether it could grow to its full stature as a church until it acquired wealth and political influence, by which it was able to establish a structure of the sacred more impressive than the structures of Judaism and Hellenistic-Roman paganism. The question is whether the church, established by Jesus Christ as Christian, needed Constantine in order to become a church.

These thoughts come to mind when one reads Roman documents suggesting that the sacred personnel be more certainly defined by their garb and their manner of life. If we need this apparatus of the sacred to do something which the apostolic church did better without, it is possible that the religious garb and manner of life are a substitute for something which the apostolic church had and we lack. A Roman document which would identify this factor would be useful. To paraphrase a hymn which is not one of my favorites, they shall know we are Christians by our garb. And those who do not wear the garb? Well, sit down for a minute and let me explain. Sacred personnel, you see, do the work of the church; in a way they are the church. . . .

*Chapter Six*

# ACADEMIA VS. SECRECY IN THE CHURCH

IT USED be to a standard feature of sermon form and style, which I abandoned years ago, to introduce the discourse with a text. This is not a sermon, I hope, but I am going to give a text. It comes from John 18:19-22, and reads thus in the Revised Standard Version: "The high priest then questioned Jesus about his disciples and his teaching. Jesus answered him, 'I have spoken openly to the world; I have always taught in synagogues and in the temple, where all Jews come together; I have said nothing secretly. Why do you ask me? Ask those who have heard me what I said to them; they know what I said.' When he had said this, one of the officers standing by struck Jesus with his hand." I included the last sentence because the response of the officer may suggest a common attitude toward a man who hints that he does not set great value on secrecy. Let me reassure my colleagues and others that I am well aware that the matter is not as simple as it appears, and that the three other Gospels have things like private instructions given to the disciples and commands not to publish the statement that Jesus was the Messiah. To put these together would take more than a chapter, and the reader is safe in sharing my position that no explanation of these texts will make John 18:20-21 mean anything else but what it says. What it says is that Jesus said and did nothing which he was not willing to have submitted to public examination.

The academic man is usually blind to the values of secrecy. When he teaches, he is not so foolish as to imagine that anything presented to a class can be accompanied by an effective warning to keep the material secret. It is his business to be quoted, and the more quotable things he says the more he interests his audience, a task which he can never afford to forget. When he writes, it is of the very essence that what he writes be published; no one writes not to be published. In his academic world he is convinced that learning is best served by open and free discussion of scholars; this means that scholars do not withhold their conclusions and their opinions from each other nor from their students. Sound method and sound pedagogy may recommend that he defer presentation of material until it is in shape for publication or until his students have advanced to a point where they can understand him; but this is not secrecy. We do not keep integral calculus secret from six-graders although we do not teach it to them. In the world of learning it is impossible to think of any good purpose which secrecy will serve.

No doubt this is a blind spot, and it reflects the detachment from real life and real business which is characteristic of the scholar in the opinion of his contemporaries. I have a personal blind spot here bigger than the blind spot of my colleagues; and I would not like to have a record of the number of times when friends and associates have called me Old Blabbermouth. Secrecy is not the same thing as privacy, which I cherish rather jealously. I take baths in private, but it has not occurred to me to attempt to conceal the fact that I take them; it would disturb me if I thought this fact were secret. A letter is supposed to be a "natural" secret; but it is years since I wrote a letter without thinking of how it would look if it were published. This probably makes my later correspondence less interesting than my youthful correspondence. I would take it amiss if anyone walked into the room or the office unannounced and uninvited while I am present; but both room and office have to be in a shape which will not compromise me if the maids and the janitors come in, as they always do, when I am absent. So where is the line between secrecy and privacy? I do object to the inspection of my luggage by customs officers because it is an intrusion of my privacy—not because of anything I carry, but because I am the world's worst packer. But to inspect luggage, as they do it, in the presence of any passerby, is an intolerable intrusion of privacy; and if the Government cannot stick its nose in my bag in private, I wish it would not stick it in there at all.

Let us consider some places where secrecy is valued more than it is in the academic world; and in fact this is practically the rest of the world. Every small boy forms or joins a secret society at some time in his boyhood. Politics and business cannot move without secrecy. Some journalists exaggerate, I am sure, when they say that in Washington the routine document is "Secret," and they have run out of superlatives to describe a document which they really want to keep secret. They might try the principle of the purloined letter. I really have no information and no judgment about these things, but others do. There are things, undefined as they may be, which a government may not conceal from the citizens. A corporation must report to its stockholders; whether they understand the report is irrelevant, but the officers of the company are subject to an inquisition on their management. There are limits on the practice of secrecy, and managers who transgress them may be voted out of office—if the constituency has the voting power. Where neither election nor recall is the work of an electorate, we encounter a quite different cat. Secrecy is in history and in tradition and in popular belief associated with absolute government.

To return to the Gospel text quoted above: Whatever "the very words" of Jesus may have been, their application in the church has been restricted to the topic mentioned in the text, teaching. It has certainly not been referred to government. To give examples of secrecy is difficult, of course, for where secrecy has been effective one cannot find an example. We do hear the phrase, "the open church." How open? Let me illustrate by an example which may not seem just to the point. Almost all religious communities had two rules, sometimes nearly back to back: one forbade the subjects to inquire of superiors concerning government, and the other commanded them to submit their correspondence, both inbound and outbound, to be read by the superior. One superior was known to post sealed letters on the community bulletin board to be repossessed by the sender. It is obvious where the values of secrecy lie. Yet almost anything a superior does as superior is a matter of interest to the community; it is difficult to think that the personal correspondence of the subjects would often be of community interest, but I suppose the superior reads the mail as the representative of the community. It is hard to think of any other title by which he could think of it.

We have the now celebrated—and almost abandoned—practice of the secret prohibition of writing for publication. Not only is the prohibition secret, but the reasons for the prohibition are secret too. We have the secret letter to officers of the church, in which they are directed to take action without disclosing the directive. We even have the secret newsletter mimeographed on yellow paper with no acknowledgement of responsibility. One has to say that the "Yellow Sheet" is not entirely out of harmony with many church practices. To me an anonymous letter is cowardly, whether it is manuscript, typescript, mimeographed or embossed on vellum; but this is one of my blind spots. I am accustomed to sign my letters and my publications. I would like to sign my censors' reports too—yes, occasionally I engage in censorship—but the name would be deleted at headquarters; it is the Rule. Headquarters may be ashamed of my report, but I am not. Of course the manuscript comes in without name too. The theory here is that anonymity will protect the author from unfairness and the organization from favoritism, and will give the censor freedom to speak his mind. It also gives him freedom to forget his manners occasionally; nobody is as free as the anonymous author. If the author cannot take criticism gracefully and the censor give criticism gracefully, then the group has a sickness which anonymity will not cure. One rather celebrated religious superior instructed lower superiors that anonymous letters should be read and then destroyed; they should be ignored, but they can offer an occasion for discreet inquiry.

We can hardly enumerate the values of secrecy without mentioning the secret denunciation. No commentary on this is necessary except to read Matthew 18:15-17. Secret denunciation is so completely the opposite of the practice described in Matthew that it paralyzes discourse. This is not an ecclesiastical practice; it is a police practice. Policemen tell us that they could not maintain law and order without the stool pigeon. They may be right; I can make no judgment of this. But since church officers are not dealing with robbers, burglars, forgers, counterfeiters, smugglers, murderers (professional and amateur), pimps and dope pushers, I wonder whether they need the stool pigeon to administer the community of love—or, to forestall an objection, whether the stool pigeon will bring the community of love any nearer. For the first time in my life—and I shall not give the source in the journal where I saw it—a priest said to a reporter that his telephone was tapped. The late Arthur (Dutch Schultz) Flegenheimer used to begin every telephone conversation with the wish, "I hope your **** ears drop off." Well, it is nice to know in whose company you are put.

It is really stupid to call the United States an Anglo-Saxon country, but we do live under British and American common law. The continent of Europe lives under the tradition of Roman law, in which secret processes are accepted. The Latin word for stool pigeon is *delator,* and Tacitus wrote a great deal about the pigeons in the Roman Empire. He did not like them. He felt that it was government by corruption. Let us say that he was a bit narrow here. We have no right to impose British and American common law on another legal tradition. We may have a right to appeal to the Gospel of Matthew. We make a mistake when we simply dismiss a legal tradition which is two thousand years old, and we make an even greater mistake when we judge that those who do these things think they are doing anything wrong.

I have briefly touched on the alleged value of secrecy: that it protects the good name of the people involved. One would wish that it were no more than Jack Webb's line: "Only the names have been changed to protect the innocent." The trouble is that the innocent are not protected. To take an example: Here is the Reverend Doctor Fulgentius J. Erudite, an articulate and industrious theologian who produces an embarrassing flow of books and articles. All of a sudden the flow stops, and perhaps

Doctor Fulgentius is attached to a medical mission in Tierra del Fuego. What did he do? Is he ill? No, he is as sound as a drum. Did he hear the same call which Albert Schweitzer heard? Possibly, but he has not said so. Did he run out of ideas? Not Fulgentius; Niagara Falls will dry up first. Did he teach heresy? Well, no one has said what he did, although I read, mind you, that his books were taken out of circulation in the diocese of Nether Wallop. I spare the reader further conjectures of possible moral collapses of Fulgentius. Whatever was saved, it was not the good name of Fulgentius; what was saved was the good name of men who wanted Fulgentius shut up, but could not find the evidence to show him wrong. Fulgentius was an academic lamb lost in the jungle of administrative tigers; the poor *schlupf*, he thought his ideas should be discussed and criticized in public by his peers. He could have stood a heresy trial, and that is the reason why he did not get one. He is not innocent, he is just naive.

So we may be on the track of the values of secrecy, besides the fact that it is a game played by small boys who have not grown up. It does protect the innocent because it protects authority. It protects authority from criticism, because the development of decisions is not known. When one can only conjecture the reasons for a decision, one runs the risk of rash judgment; of course one also runs the risk of being right, but one will never know. It protects authority from discussion, because the subjects are presented with a formed decision that leaves no alternative except obedience or disobedience. It permits the use of methods of which we might be a little ashamed if they were known, but which seem absolutely necessary for the purposes of administration. And it does keep that distance between authority and the governed which permits a cool and detached attitude toward the governed, who are outside the machine. Shall we add that it contributes to the fear of the unknown? Indeed there are many values of secrecy, all of which the church would be better off without. We are moving toward an open church—not very fast, but we are moving. Once the government of the church is no longer regarded as the exclusive privilege of a ruling class, but as something in which every member has a deep concern, secrecy is dead. And this last sentence is a fair paraphrase of much which the Second Vatican Council said. I shall repeat something which I said in a book: The public is stubbornly convinced that nobody hides anything except those who have something to hide. What the church does is not something to hide.

*Chapter Seven*

# IT TAKES MORE
# THAN LARGE CROWDS

**B**Y COINCIDENCE, it seems, I have recently encountered several individual groups who said that they are in search of Christian community. When I first heard this, I was more appalled than I let on; surely this is rather late in history for Catholics to be searching for Christian community. One would think that Christian community is a basic product of the proclamation of the Gospel. But these people are not kooks and they are not ignorant and they are not inactive; if anything, they are overeducated and overactive in the church. When they attest that they are looking for Christian community, and by implication that they do not have it, they say something which ought to jar everyone who is interested in the church. The one thing I will not do is to dismiss them without listening to them. There may be others who feel a lack of Christian community, but have not the will or the way to say it.

The first thing that comes to my mind when I hear this is that for these people the parish has failed. The obvious response which any monsignor could make is that the parish has not failed them; they have failed the parish. For a good many of them I can attest personally that this is not the answer; and even if it were, the further question is who failed whom first? We learned in Chicago a few years ago that some of our parishes are not Christian communities. We learned also that they are not Christian communities because the parishioners do not wish them to be Christian communities. My opinion, for what it is worth, is that these parishes and others which feel the same way should decently withdraw from the Roman Catholic communion. But my acquaintances do not come from such pseudo-parishes as these; and while the study of the social pathology of such parishes may help us to understand the failure of the parish elsewhere, I suspect the failure goes wider and deeper.

Those who seek Christian community have sometimes tried to find it by assembling groups of similar background and similar interests. I warned them that they may be forming an elite group, and I loathe Christian elite groups. They are aware of this danger, but they say that they act from desperation. They are convinced that the parish is beyond redemption. But a community has to be structured—loosely rather than rigidly, perhaps, but structured. They have not found another structure. Much of the problem lies in the mobile urban world. Men work in one place and live in another; the husband has one set of community relationships in his employment, his wife another set in the place of residence, the family as a whole still another. I have no desire to restore the village culture in which one social reality embraced all relations; the village is narrow by definition. But the urban community seems sometimes to replace one narrow social scheme by several. We are all members of several communities, which sometimes seem to meet only at the point of our membership. Each of them can and does show the village mentality. The parish does not fail simply because we no longer live in villages, but this has something to do with it.

D. W. Brogan once wrote that American Protestants are frightened by the large crowds which they see at the Catholic church on Sunday. At a Protestant church this would be an infallible sign of the personal power and prestige of the minister, and it is this which elicits Protestant fear. Nothing of the sort, Mr. Brogan assured his fellow Protestants. Catholics believe that there are a number of essential spiritual services which they can obtain only at the parish church; and a crowd at the Catholic church is no more a sign of the power of the priest than a crowd at the post office is a sign of the power of the postmaster. Brogan may have hit it; for us Catholics the parish is the spiritual post office, the spiritual supermarket, the spiritual movie house or bowling parlor; and we have the same community as the customers at the post office or the A & P. We may even have the community of the passengers on the Evanston Express—all going to the same place by the same means without knowing each other or being concerned with each other.

No doubt the unbiblical theology of the sacraments as individual means of grace has something to do with this; the parish church is also the spiritual pharmacy. The sacraments as symbols of the encounter of the community with God and of the members with each other are not well understood. I suspect that much of the opposition to the use of the vernacular comes from the fact that it is impossible to conceal the symbolism of the community if the vernacular is used; those who do not wish to have community do not wish to have it ritually symbolized. One high-ranking ecclesiastic has vigorously objected to the handshake as a symbol of the "Pax." If you will pardon the illustration, it is something like keeping the Canon in whispered Latin. Whispered Latin bothers no one; but if the celebrant, using the words of Jesus, announces clearly and in English, "Take this and drink it, all of you; this is the chalice of my blood," and then does not give the cup, the disparity between the original institution and current practice becomes so clear as to be uncomfortable. The litniks believe that an authentic liturgy will go far to restore community; with perhaps less enthusiasm than theirs, I support their moves toward an authentic liturgy. It will at least make it more difficult to deny community.

Why should the parish not be a basis of community? As we know the parish, it is identical with a neighborhood; and neighborhood seems to be one of the elements of community. One of the strengths of Chicago is supposed to be the vigor of its neighborhood community organizations. In the fragmentation of communities of the modern city the neighborhood remains one of the sturdier groups. Integration, to take a random example, goes much better in business and industry than it does in residence. A man and his family still live where their home is, and I judge they still fight for it. It is certainly strange that a city neighborhood should be more of a community than a parish is; yet this seems to happen.

Someone has said that the city parish of 1990 will be in a store. The clergy will live in the back of the store or in a loft, the store will be open 24 hours a day, the clergy will walk the streets and know everyone in the neighborhood by his or her first name. It is an interesting projection—probably no more and no less accurate than other prophecies—and states much more clearly what the present parish lacks than what the future parish will be. I would like to say here, because it has to be said somewhere in this piece, that when we talk about the survival of the parish we are talking about the survival of the church; the question is not trivial. The church of 1990 expresses impatience with vast expensive mausoleums (in deference to the editor: the correct plural is *mausolea*), with parish populations too large or too dense, with the withdrawal of the clergy from the life of their people. It may even express impatience with the attention and revenue devoted to the parochial school; it may be said that the parish frequently serves its children better than it serves its adults. Why should it not serve both?

Would the store church be more of a community? To the extent that it would correct some of the defects of the existing parish structure, it could be; but by itself it does not touch what may be the heart of the problem. I suggest that the parish is not a Christian community because it is a Catholic community; and by limiting itself to the Catholic community it fails to be a community at all. We Catholics form elite groups within our neighborhood; we are the good vs. the bad, the holy vs. the wicked, the saved vs. the damned. We are the in-group to end all in-groups. We help our own, if we help anyone, but we are not in the business of helping any outsiders. Did the mythological headline ever appear in the Catholic press: "100 Die in Fire; No Catholics"? Among the charges laid against Christians in the Roman Empire was *odium generis humani*, hatred of the human race. If the early Christians were very much like us, we may have been unfair to some of the persecutors. We seem to have read Matthew 5:43 ("You have heard it said: Love your neighbor, and hate your enemy") without going on to read 5:44. Our parishes are closed societies, and that is why they are not Christian communities. The Christian community is an open society by definition; its outlook is as broad as the outlook of Jesus Christ, who died to save all men. We have much in common with the Pharisees, to whom also we are often unfair; at least it seems unfair to traduce those from whom one has borrowed so much.

How are we to open this society? This is not a matter of organization and structure; it is a matter of persons. What have to be opened are minds. It means more than the fact that the church is open to anyone; we all know this, but openness means more than a readiness to accept converts. It means a readiness to accept those who are not converts. We accept them as persons, as those who Jesus has said are identified with him, as those in whom we find God. Our concern touches the entire community, not just its Catholic members. There is still room in our society to feed the hungry, clothe the naked, and harbor the harborless; at least we can make it possible for them to obtain these things, and not stand in the way. If we cannot achieve community within our neighborhood, it seems very doubtful that we can achieve community with those more remote. We have long been more ready to help heathens and the poor in Asia and Africa than we are to help heathens and the poor in our own cities. The Asians and Africans do not ruin the neighborhood as long as they stay in Asia and Africa.

One has to ask whether clerical leadership has anything to do with the lack of community. No doubt it has, but neither the space nor the material is available to discuss it fully here. It can hardly be that there are too few clergy, since so much of the world has even fewer clergy than we have. It may have something to do with the distribution of the clergy and with the extraneous duties which so often lie upon them. If the clergy are plant-minded, school-minded, money-minded, rather than people-minded, it is because they have inherited the type of parish which they operate. High church leadership has often shown these attributes, and it communicates its values to the lower clergy. Christian community is the result of a deep concern with persons, all persons within one's reach, not just the elect. The clergy generally have not been trained to create Christian community; they have been trained to manage the spiritual supermarket. Their engagement with those outside the fold is "convert work." No slur on lay leadership and lay activity is intended when I say that the Christian community will not arise without clerical leadership.

Will it arise at all? Some reflection on this question leads one to wonder how often the church has ever achieved Christian community. Once the question is raised, one suspects that it has rarely been achieved. The church has achieved things which look like Christian community but which were not. Historic "Christendom" was rather a huge mockery of Christian community. It was the biggest in-group community of the elect which the church has ever had, and we look back to it with regret. Perhaps no more was possible in that world. But a new vision of Christian community is possible and necessary now. The church has to identify herself with men, not with men plus cultural and ethnic adjectives. She is no more than faithful to her origins and her best traditions when she does this. She has to do it in parishes, because this is where the people are.

I have said that clerical leadership is necessary. But clerical leadership does respond to lay demands. It certainly has responded in many parishes which are not Christian communities. The layman who seeks Christian community should not wait until the clerical leader comes along. The layman can compel him to appear. He will have to show his clergy that he is there to be led in the direction of Christian community. This demand must be met. Some have expressed apprehension that groups such as those I mentioned at the opening of this chapter will simply withdraw from clerical leadership. I do not mean that they will withdraw into heresy or schism; this would be too old-fashioned. I mean that they will lose confidence in clerical leadership or counsel. The danger is not that the hierarchy and the clergy will be disobeyed, but simply that they may become unimportant. I cannot say whether this danger is near. All I know is that if I were a bishop or a pastor, it would worry me.

*Chapter Eight*

# REVOLUTION AND THE
# CHURCH OF THE
# STATUS QUO

I AM AWARE that any other country in the world which had so many and such massive civil disturbances as the United States would be thought to be in a revolution. And perhaps that is just where we are. It is not a question of the numbers involved; it is hard to think of any revolution which was not pulled off by a determined and organized minority, more often than not a very small minority. The revolutionary minority has not always kept control of the movement which it started, but the revolution once started continues, in the same hands or in other hands.

Now what business has a theologian, even a theological journalist, to inflict his thoughts on revolution upon his devoted if limited public? He cannot be more than an amateur student of the theory of revolutions, and as yet there is no theology of revolution. Enough people have commented on the events to make further comments unnecessary. But the theologian can have a deeply personal interest in revolution. He can remember that the Roman Catholic Church has been involved in every revolution which has occurred where the church was present; and he may remember that in every revolution the church was identified with the *status quo*, the *ancien régime*, or whatever it was which the revolution destroyed. His reflections as a theologian might begin right there; but before they do, let us try a little amateur preliminary work on the theory of revolutions.

I understand a revolution to mean the violent overthrow of institutions; and if anyone boggles at the word "violent," I observe that we ought to have another word for changes which are not violent. Institutions being what they are, it is nearly impossible to overthrow them except by violence. My definition is negative, and I mean it that way; the revolution deliberately sets out to destroy, not to build; or if it begins with plans to build, the violence which it initiates nearly always means that these plans will be replaced by others before the revolution runs its course. The revolution comes when enough people find the situation so intolerable that they will no longer suffer either the situation or the institutions which they blame for the situation; and as we have already observed, this need be no more than a small minority. The small minority can wreck the institutions even if it cannot replace them. You can think of this minority as a kind of critical mass; until it reaches sufficient magnitude, there is still time for the institutions to correct the intolerable situation, or for the dissatisfied to get satisfaction by means other than violence.

One can observe also that a revolution can advance some distance before it is recognized as a revolution. Among the first things to go in any revolution are the moderates—and this helps to make my own interest intensely personal. The revolutionary minority is not in a controlling position, or it would not be revolutionary; but the fear it engenders brings power to the moderates. The moderates disappear either by ceasing to be moderates or by being annihilated along with the conservatives; for they become the major obstacle to the revolution in its early phases simply by their proposals to correct the intolerable situation without destroying the institutions.

Let me add to these fragments of theory the statement that I do not see how any sane man can look forward to a revolution as the cure of social evils; it seems he would know little about the history of revolutions. One has to say that no matter what the revolution accomplishes, there must be a better way of doing it. Some of the things which perish with the moderates are certain basic canons of morality and human decency. Persons cease to be persons and become symbols. Nevertheless, the revolution seems to be as inevitable as war, because man is really not what Aristotle and the Scholastics defined him to be, a rational animal. The revolution meets violence with violence until the community is sick of it and decides to make a stab at rationality. I am as well aware as any literate citizen of certain inequities not only in the United States but also in other countries; and one may be explicit enough to mention Latin America in a general way. For both the United States and for Latin America the revolutionary minority may be approaching the critical mass; surely few revolutions have occurred with more provocation on the part of the institutions. The prospect still makes one sick.

H. Rap Brown said that violence is as American as cherry pie. The statement needs correction on two counts. First, he should have said apple pie. Secondly, he should have said white violence; we Caucasians have never admitted the right of the black man, the red man, the yellow man, or the brown man to block the march of white civilization by the use of violence. I do not think Mr. Brown knows how violent the white man is, and he ought to know it better than I do. I can support the thesis that the United States of America is the most violent nation in recorded history, including such thugs as the Assyrians, the Romans, and the much overrated Mongols and Tartars. No nation has ever killed so many people, citizens and aliens, in so short a time. We have inherited all the violent traditions of Europe together with our own violent traditions of the frontier; and if one goes back beyond the United States proper to the colonies from which the nation arose, the tradition is there from the beginning. Quite early in the history of New England a small Indian tribe named the Pequots, or Pequods, showed some resentment at the fact that white men moved into what the Pequots unreasonably regarded as their territory. The American Indians had nothing like the European tradition of violence, but they were not unacquainted with primitive forms of violence which they used to express their resentment. The God-fearing men of Massachusetts exterminated the Pequots, man, woman, and child, and set the style for the treatment of the Amerind which was maintained, although rarely with such austere perfection, until 1890.

"The American way" to resolve differences between man and man, whether singly or in groups, has been to bash in the heads of the disagreeing persons or party. This runs through such quaint episodes as the Whisky Rebellion; it runs through the history of labor organizations, the building of railroads and industries, the mythology of the shoot-out at sundown, and through our various wars, as well. As far as the shoot-out is concerned, there is probably as much gunplay any given night in Los Angeles as there was in a year in Dodge City when Wyatt Earp and Bat Masterson upheld law and order. Many metropolitan policemen have easily and notably surpassed Earp's claim that he shot three men dead in his entire career, including the encounter at the OK Corral. Possibly the frontier was more peaceful when the Sioux were buffalo nomads in Kansas than when Smith and Hickock invaded Holcomb. Certainly the buffalo were safer with the Sioux, and one thinks the Clutters might have been too.

That the white American has turned soft or civilized in these later days I do not believe. It is customary—with apologies to the Jews—to call this nation a Christian country. The statement is so manifestly false that one does not know how to frame the denial. If anyone counts on the Christian beliefs and habits of white Americans to restrain their violence, forget it. There is a little-known piece by Mark Twain called "The War Prayer" which both the limits of space and the desires of the editors for original contributions forbid me from putting here in its fullness. Mark was also as American as apple pie, by no stretch of the imagination subversive except that he was an unbeliever; and that should not hurt his reputation in our age. The piece is such an acid satire on those who pray that God will bless our arms that I think no clergyman could read it and pray for victory again without choking on the words. Mark understood the Christianity he rejected better than some who profess it; it was his insight that they had never accepted it which drove him to repudiate it.

Where does all this lead? It leads me to conclude that the United States cannot afford a revolution. Everything suggests that it would make previous revolutions look like tea and cookies in the garden. The price of freeing ourselves from our own demon of violence could be the mutual extermination of the violent, and with them most of the nonviolent. U. S. Grant was once asked how long he thought the Civil War would continue. He said, in the authentic American way, until the Southern slave-owning aristocracy were killed off. That was very nearly the way it happened; the slave-owning aristocracy were excellent representatives of the American way, and they would accept no other solution.

I began this as a theological essay; and it is time to ask where the Catholic Church stands. We do not know that the revolution is inevitable; we do know that unless certain things are done and done quickly, the critical mass will be reached. The church, we said, has always been with the *status quo,* which is not as harsh as it sounds; it has always stood for law and order because it cannot stand for lawlessness and disorder. But when law and order institutionalize injustice, what can the church say? It has rarely had a prophetic voice in this situation. Its position at the moment is ambiguous because the church may face an internal revolution—in an improper sense, as I take the term; but lack of unity means that she sounds an uncertain trumpet. She is further compromised by the fact that the church, effectively if not formally, has accepted violence as long as it is used by governments. She has remained silent in our recent orgasm of violence in Vietnam. We are led by a President who seems bent on reincarnating the legendary Texas gunmen, except that these legendary Texans handled their own gun work. We had found a problem in Vietnam—or shall we say that we had created one? And we had no way to solve this problem except the traditional American way: kill the bastards. How can the church tell people not to solve domestic problems in the traditional American way?

I do not imply that the church is idle in what may be a domestic crisis. Many priests and laymen are engaged in wholesome activities which are intended to keep the situation from becoming intolerable. But the church has not massed her influence under official leadership in these activities. We ought now to be able to realize that we have not done what we could have done, and that is to proclaim the commandment of love, the commandment which might arrest revolution and its causes. The proclamation of law and order arrests neither. When the prophets of ancient Israel spoke to their people, they did not address the poor and oppressed at all; their speech was directed entirely to the oppressors. The oppressors did not give them much attention, but the words were aimed in the only direction which could be effective. In the gospels likewise Jesus does not attack oppression by saying that oppression is inevitable. Jesus was killed by the ruling classes, not by the masses; yet he cannot be called a revolutionary in the proper sense, because his message consistently is that violence solves no human problems. The church can hardly improve on his message; but has the church even succeeded in uttering his message? Unless she matches her proclamation of patience to the poor by a proclamation of self-abandoment to others, she is not proclaiming the whole gospel; and somehow part of the gospel has no meaning.

Actually I fear that a revolution is inevitable in our country because the country has earned it. Our history of violence has placed us under God's judgment; and one may wonder whether there are ten righteous men in Sodom for whose sake God might avert the judgment.

*Chapter Nine*

# RADICAL EVIL AND SIN

I HAVE not the clipping ready at hand, but I believe it was a French bishop, on the occasion of the statement of the French hierarchy on contraception, who distinguished between evil acts and sinful acts. Some things—I paraphrase—are evil but not sinful. The bishop admitted that he had killed four Germans when he was a member of the underground resistance. This was evil, he said, but not sinful. He went on to apply the principle to contraception, which he saw as evil but not necessarily as sinful. This is more than a standard cliché about the necessary evil that men must do. It struck me that the bishop had put his finger on something which in this chapter I shall call radical evil; but the distinction between radical evil and sin is more subtle than the bishop's statement implies. I do not intend to pass a moral judgment either on contraception or on killing Germans, but I do not think either moral problem can be solved by distinguishing evil from sin. Scholastic philosophy has long distinguished moral evil, which is sinful, from physical evil, which is not; this distinction also does not seem adequate to reality.

Radical evil includes original sin, in whatever sense the term is understood. Radical evil is cosmic evil, "the principalities and powers, the world rulers of this darkness, the spiritual wicked things on high" (Ephesians 6:12). Radical evil is Satan and his devils. Radical evil is the beast or the demonic in man, known in theological language as concupiscence. All of these express the

73

conviction that evil is bigger than man, that it is not under his control, that it is present whether man does it or not; and this is what I mean by radical evil. I will add to this list Paul's coupling of Sin and Death, to which he is enslaved (Romans 5-7); his slavery does not allow him to do the good which he wishes. It is the coupling of Sin and Death which makes it possible to include this passage under the heading radical evil. Death is inevitable.

Years ago Reinhold Niebuhr defined the traditional belief in original sin as belief in man's "creatureliness." There was never a fall; man's "sin" consists simply in the fact that man is not God, that he has powers which he can never realize. Man's reach exceeds his grasp; one might paraphrase Niebuhr by saying that man is a born loser. This also is an appeal to radical evil. By stretching a point one could include under the heading Luther's view of men as hopelessly sinful and Calvin's predestination.

Radical evil furnishes most of the plots of the theater and the novel. These plots portray man as falling into radical evil by doing what he must. We all know after a certain number of years that, rather than a clear choice between good and evil, more frequently we have a choice of evils. Radical evil is Hamlet killing his stepfather or, to fall to a lower literary level, the Virginian meditating, as he buckles on his gun for the shootout with Trampas, that there is nothing else he can do. We learn from experience that we are the prisoners of our past choices. Every time we make a decision we remove an unknown number of future choices from our freedom. Radical evil includes our own commitments as well as the commitments which others impose upon us. To reverse a way of life is simply not to be expected; it does happen, but we do not count on it.

Yet we are inconsistent. We draw a line without knowing exactly where or why we drew it. We accepted Hiroshima and Nagasaki, we accepted Vietnam, but we refuse Hitler's final solution. We will say that he was a wicked man, not merely that he did a wicked thing. Is radical evil measured by quantity? It seems to me that once we allow men to do radical evil under compulsion there is no line we can draw. The principle of radical evil leaves room for Hitler, just as it leaves room for Hiroshima and the assassins of the underground. Short stories are usually shallow, but I read one about Algerian terrorists which made my blood run cold. What chilled me was that the terrorists of the story were intolerably self-righteous; I suppose they have to be to do what they do. *Time* magazine's movie reviewer described one of the characters in *Exodus* as "a saintly old assassin." These and all like them, historical or fictitious, were doing what they thought they had to do; and one can conclude only that men's judgment of what they have to do is not readily to be trusted.

Radical evil is war, it is poverty and disease, it is all the human suffering which ultimately is caused by men. It is also such things as earthquakes and windstorms. I deliberately group things attributed to men with things attributed to nature because, if I think biblically, I may understand all of these things as God's judgments. When Jesus was asked about eighteen men who were killed by a falling tower, he said that you will perish in the same way unless you repent. Repent of radical evil? Before we attack this, let us recall a few other sayings of Jesus.

The parables of the Good Samaritan and of Dives and Lazarus place before us not men who are guilty but men who chose not to get involved. I have my own memories of occasions in which I did not get involved, and they are not pleasant memories. In every instance there were genuine obstacles to involvement; and one has to tell oneself that the obstacles were insuperable. Were they, really? Did not one on other occasions and perhaps for quite other motives overcome obstacles which looked as difficult? Like the Good Samaritan, we have to make such decisions quickly; there is no time to weigh the probabilities. We act by instinct, or we pass by. Some of us should have highly disciplined instincts, and we are worse when we pass by. Radical evil is created not so much by what we do as by what we fail to do. We stand by, we keep silent, we say it is the way of the world. About radical evil we are generally cynical; because we are, people continue to die of war, of starvation, of exposure, of violence and crime. We do not condone these things; we simply believe that nothing can be done, and that those who try to do something upset the uneasy balance in which we survive.

Now to return to the question: can we repent of radical evil? I can only ask questions here, because theology is not well enough formed to permit assertions. Is it not radical evil from which Jesus liberates us? When Paul speaks of liberation from Sin and Death, does he not mean that man incorporated into Christ has been endowed with power against radical evil? And if man has not been so endowed, then from what has he been liberated? No Christian conception of God can include divine complacency about radical evil. But man is complacent, and to that extent he fails to be one with God. Radical evil is man's excuse for the wicked things he does or tolerates. One could almost write a demonstration of the necessary existence of radical evil, after the manner of Thomas Aquinas. We quote the saying of Jesus that the poor we have always with us. Let us quote the whole saying: and when you wish, you may do good to them. It is, after all, a form of direct action against radical evil.

A great deal of Christian theology and Christian practice is a surrender to radical evil, and I suggest that this is an implicit denial of the efficacy of the redemption. The world goes on as if the Christ-event had never happened. Quite often we postpone radical evil to the eschatological end-time; that is, we leave it to God. It is his problem, so to speak, not ours. If Jesus has really liberated us from radical evil, some of us are going to be surprised in the eschatological end-time; Jesus is quoted as saying just about that in Matthew 25: 31-46. We also enjoy radical evil as a crutch for our moral failings. A parent once told me about a precocious son who pleaded that he should not be punished because he was only a little boy who did not know any better. The parent felt that a child intelligent enough to enter the plea—which was really a plea of radical evil—was intelligent enough to be punished. Radical evil is our way of life. We fear to replace it with radical good.

I ask also whether Jesus did not annihilate the distinction between sin and radical evil; whether he admitted that there is any radical evil other than sin; whether he did not teach that man by overcoming sin overcomes radical evil; whether he did not teach that man by surrendering to radical evil surrenders to sin. To stick to our two parables, the good Samaritan could not wipe out banditry on the Jericho road nor could Dives have conducted single-handed a war on poverty. The one is praised for doing what was within his grasp, and the other is damned for not doing what was within his grasp. The good Samaritan is a classic figure because we recognize that he is atypical and has to be fictitious. Dives, unfortunately, is quite typical and quite real. One may conclude that radical evil remains, that man is still the slave of sin, unless enough people are determined not to accept radical evil wherever they encounter it. It seems to have been in the mind of Jesus that if he started a small group with this conviction, the idea would spread until it became dominant. Since the idea has so much merit, it is not surprising that the original group was so enthusiastic about it. What ever happened to it?

I suggest also that radical evil easily approaches some form of dualism, which Christianity claims to reject. There are many forms of dualism, but they all ultimately affirm that evil is a positive principle of reality. To suggest that radical evil is indestructible approaches making it a positive principle. To say that it remains untouched by the saving act of God in Christ approaches turning it into a positive principle. I say approaches, because Christian belief and Christian thinking about this problem have never been entirely consistent; and you have to say this for most dualists, they are consistent. Much of the time we escape dualism by getting under the eschatological umbrella; and this approaches a confession that the world is really the kingdom of Satan, not the kingdom of God. Effectively we doubt that the Christian presence in the world can do anything about radical evil.

Most theologians who speculate about evil fall flat on their faces and I may be doing it too; I shall not notice it until my nose bleeds. They fall because evil is the supreme irrational with which one cannot deal rationally. Speak of evil in its own terms and you have lost the argument. Jesus did not deal with it rationally. At the risk of simplifying his teaching, I shall say that his response to evil is that it ought not be, it need not be, and it will not be if man, adopted into divine sonship, wills with the power God has given him that it shall not be. Some wit has said that God so loved the world that he did not send a committee. Neither did Jesus send a committee; he put the response to radical evil squarely on each individual believer.

Occasionally I hear from some of my younger contemporaries that Catholicism turns them off. Recalling that I was probably as self-righteous and patronizing at their age as they are now, I swallow my indignation and attempt to be sweetly reasonable. But there are some questions I hope they will not ask me, and one is this: does one need to be a Roman Catholic in order to learn how to compromise with evil? It seems to be my duty to tell them that this is not Roman Catholicism, and only a narrow experience of Roman Catholicism makes them think that it is.

## Chapter Ten

# GIANT STEPS FORWARD–
# AND BACKWARD

F OR SOME reason, not only I but almost all of my colleagues in exegesis let 1968 slip by without a proper com-
memoration of the twenty-fifth anniversary of *Divino Afflante Spiritu*, issued in 1943. There is some coincidence, not
without irony, in this inattention. The encyclical was published
during the darkest days of the Second World War, and it was
difficult either to understand the Pope's concern with exegesis
or to share it. In addition, news of Vatican activity was published more slowly in 1943. No doubt some would say now that
concern with exegesis should have been matched by concern
with the prospects of Jews in concentration camps. The concern
with exegesis is a matter of public record; concern with the Jews
is not and will not become a matter of public record in my
lifetime. Our forgetting the anniversary was due to a different
cause. We forgot about *Divino Afflante Spiritu* because we were
excited about another encyclical which seemed to move in the
opposite direction. It is this excitement which justifies a memo-
rial service for *Divino Afflante Spiritu*.

In the first decade of the twentieth century the Roman See
engaged in a bitter conflict with a theological movement called
Modernism. Although it was probably unplanned, the issue of
this conflict was that the Roman See firmly rejected almost all
the biblical scholarship of the preceding century. A total rejec-

79

tion of this scholarship was as uncritical as its total acceptance. The pontifical documents which condemned Modernism turned theology in that direction which has come to be called "Roman," the theology which surfaced in such an alarming manner at the Second Vatican Council. Biblical scholarship was an exception; it had been freed from Roman theology in 1943, and by 1962 it had achieved an identity of its own. It has also won an acceptance in the church which rendered it safe from the kind of attack experienced by such theologians as de Lubac, Congar, Murray and Rahner. Biblical scholarship has been given more credit than it really deserves as a factor in renewal and reform; but biblical scholarship is respected and influential because it is free from Roman restraint. We may as well make this as clear as we can.

It must be understood that the tone set in the documents of Pius X condemning Modernism was maintained in the pontificates of Benedict XV and Pius XI. No statement was issued during these years which was not negative. Warnings against the dangers inherent in biblical studies came a dime a dozen between 1905 and 1940. Biblical studies are suspect; they exhibit critical methods, less than due respect for tradition and the magisterium, and they unsettle the faith of the simple. Several books were condemned for reasons not clear either then or now.

When this writer learned that his religious superiors had destined him for biblical studies, he was seriously warned by some fellow religious, both older and younger, against accepting the assignment without reservations; the reason they gave was that biblical studies in the Catholic Church were a dead end. In fact, I do not know why I accepted; after all these years I have forgotten, except that there must have been something attractive about a field of endeavor in which no movement was possible except up.

Thus let the perceptive reader understand that when we first heard of *Divino Afflante Spiritu* our reaction was: he cannot mean it, he is not serious, there must be a catch to it, the encyclical is spurious. There was a catch to it; the catch was the number of cardinals, bishops, priests and laity who were convinced that the Pope was not serious. I would estimate now that, as I remember it, it was not until 1953 that it became clear that the encyclical had wrought a change. *Humani Generis* of 1950 (not to be confused with *Humanae Vitae* of 1968) was a backlash which had no effect. By 1955 the change was clear; biblical scholars used methods condemned in earlier pontificates to reach conclusions condemned in earlier pontificates.

It was, I may say, an excellent example of the manner in which the ordinary magisterium can reverse itself without actually appearing to do so. Many biblical scholars recognized in 1943 that from that date earlier encyclicals and directives of the Biblical Commission should be ignored in their work. The problem was no more than a problem of stating this in an inoffensive way. Since 1955, at least, everyone in the field has known this. Monsignor Vaillanc could cite this as an instance in which the church moved serenely from one certainty to another.

How this came about deserves more inquiry than one can find in published material. I have heard the names of both Bea and Voste mentioned in connection with the encyclical; I have never been assured that either man was directly concerned with its composition. Both are dead, and those who know have never published their information. It is known that the body of priests engaged in biblical scholarship were quite unhappy with the restraints under which they lived. One older colleague, now deceased, had suffered some pain because of his fidelity to the restraints; in spite of this, he was simply unable to believe that the encyclical meant what it said. Others were less docile. Until the history of this affair is written we shall not know how this pressure was exercised upon the Holy See.

We who are old enough to remember when Protestants did not take Catholic scholarship seriously are uncomfortable with the memory. We are not uncomfortable because the Protestants were unfair; we are uncomfortable because they were fair. Occasionally words like dishonesty were whispered; occasionally Catholic scholars were dishonest. They affirmed things which they did not believe were true.

Let those who think that this is a healthy condition of religion and scholarship stand up and say so instead of mouthing platitudes about the beauty of submission to duly constituted authority. It is not always beautiful, and in fact one begins to think that the beautiful here is the rare and the exceptional.

I have said elsewhere, but I cannot even verify my own references, that the type of obedience admired and practiced in the Roman Catholic Church degrades both those who command and those who obey. My experience is limited to the degradation of those who obey. I wish someone with wider experience would write with clarity and conviction about the degradation of those who command, those who are ready and willing to use dishonesty and mendacity to achieve their ends when honesty and veracity will not achieve them.

One looks back on the post-Modernist period now with a kind of horror—not the horror with which one views the Inquisition, for we are not dealing with death and torture. We are dealing with the kind of horror described by Koestler and Orwell, and I do not wish this to be taken as an exaggeration. I think of one acquaintance, now long dead, who was pilloried in the reviews because he wrote not what he thought was true but what he thought the church wanted him to say and might anathematize him for not saying. Some may think this is beautiful; it makes me sick.

Now I want to assert clearly and unambiguously that it was a pontifical document which liberated the church from this pathology in one area. In that generation the scholars could not have freed themselves without a pontifical manifesto. Perhaps it was unhealthy that a manifesto was needed, and perhaps in the near future conditions will have changed enough to make such a manifesto unnecessary. It is obvious that this change has not occurred just yet. But in 1943 it happened that a pontifical document was a document of enlightenment and liberation, an instrument of reconciliation, and a factor in the renewal of learning within the church. In the Roman Catholic structure it was true in 1943, and I would hazard it is true in 1973, that the Pope can do things which no one else can do. It could be worth remembering now that the popes have sometimes done them.

After thirty years it is possible to evaluate the effects of *Divino Afflante Spiritu* for the church at large, and not merely for the practitioners of exegesis. I have not heard anyone say lately that the biblical movement has been a disaster for the church, that it has weakened faith and morals. In fact we exegetes in the present context look like sober-sided conservatives. I need not agree with some overenthusiastic appraisals of the movement; my question is whether the apprehensions expressed in the 40s and even in the 50s had any justification.

It could be instructive as well as amusing to resuscitate some of the dire predictions about biblical scholarship uttered in those days. Once the historical reality of Adam and Eve is questioned, the reality of Jesus Christ is doubted next. If I cannot believe in the Deluge, what is left in which I can believe? I am aware that some of my colleagues have proposed interpretations of the resurrection narratives which frighten some of the simple; I think their faith is as solid as the faith of the simple, at least those of the simple who throw rocks through the windows of Negro homes; and I have to trust them to examine and criticize their methods and conclusions. I do know that they will leave me free to examine and criticize, and that is all a scholar needs and desires. But I have never thought the saving event of the resurrection is so well understood that there is nothing more to say about it.

I began by contrasting *Divino Afflante Spiritu* with an encyclical which seemed to move in the opposite direction. Much has been said about *Humanae Vitae,* but I have not heard it called by anyone a document of enlightenment, liberation and reconciliation. Perhaps our short term response does not do justice to it; there were those who thought *Divino Afflante Spiritu* was a disaster. Theologians, professional and amateur, are asking what an encyclical is. We appear uncertain. It seems safe now to say that an encyclical is a contemporary statement. It initiates a discussion or a course of action which cannot be finally evaluated by those who are involved. There are certain limits to its effectiveness, limits which no one has defined and probably no one can.

My own recollection is that *Divino Afflante Spiritu* was less strongly supported by the hierarchy and the Roman Curia than

*Humanae Vitae* is supported by the same bodies. The reaction of theologians was mixed, but perhaps more theologians supported *Divino Afflante Spiritu.* Most people in the church did not even know the issues in *Divino Afflante Spiritu;* they know and they care about the issues in this one. Ultimately *Divino Afflante Spiritu* wrought a change in the area of its concern because it was so eminently reasonable and in touch with the movements of history, even if it was a belated touch. No encyclical is the last word when it is uttered; it is under the judgment of history, and it is open to another encyclical.

*Chapter Eleven*

# MISSION: TO PREACH
# NONMISSION: TO THEOLOGIZE

**L**ET ME state at the outset my thesis: the church has no commission to engage in theology. To repeat and expand: the church has not the kind of commission for theology which it has for the proclamation of the gospel, nor can it have in theology the kind of authority which it has in the proclamation of the gospel. The thesis stands on two grounds. One is the absence of any commission, explicit or implicit, derived from the New Testament to engage in theology. This needs no discussion; it is important only to notice that a valid commission has to be derived from the New Testament. The second of the two grounds is drawn from a consideration of the nature of theology; when this discipline is examined closely, it becomes evident that the church can have no commission to theologize with authority.

Let me anticipate an objection that the church needs to theologize in order to fulfill its commission to proclaim the gospel. Allowing the statement to stand unchallenged for the moment (all my colleagues in theology will recognize a transmission, which means I may attack it later), this shows no commission. Since earliest times the church has judged that it needed to own property in order to fulfill its commission, in spite of some New Testament texts which are far more easily interpreted as a prohibition of owning property than as a commission to own it.

It has judged for almost as long that it needs a Roman Curia; so far, at least, no one has affirmed that the Curia is of divine institution. The principle that the church needs something, if properly applied, shows only that, other things being equal (that it is basically moral, for instance), it is legitimate for the church to have it or to do it; it does not show that it has a commission in the technical sense to have it or to do it. My thesis is not that the church may not engage in theology, but only that it may not engage in it with authority.

In order that the nonmission of theologizing may be clearly perceived, let us state what the church is commissioned to do. The New Testament phrase for the mission is "the proclamation of the gospel." "Teach," used in Matthew 28:19, is an ancient mistranslation of a word which means "make disciples," make believers. Not even in Matthew, which uses even more Jewish phrases than Paul, is the church ever described as a school; it is a community of faith. The content of the gospel is the object of faith; in the New Testament it is faith that Jesus is Messiah and Lord who died for our sins and rose that we might be made righteous. The formula of the gospel has grown as its content and its implications were better understood. The apostles' creed is an early expression which the church still uses. Whatever be the formula employed, the church has never understood its mission of proclamation (or preaching) to cover anything but what the church believes. What it believes it must preach; and it is empowered to preach only what it believes. What it believes it proclaims with that authority which commands assent, for what it believes is the word of God.

The thesis of a nonmission to theologize makes a distinction between faith and theology; the church itself accepts such a distinction. A consideration of what theology is, I said, will show that the commission to preach does not include a mission to theologize. Theology is not easy to define, for its history shows many variations in its content and method. Perhaps no description which covers all its forms is possible other than to call it the attempt to understand what is believed by the application of human learning. Theology does not create faith, it presupposes it; theology is possible only because the church has proclaimed its belief. The understanding which theology seeks has reference to the relation of faith to human knowledge and human life. It adds nothing to the content of the gospel, but it can clarify what is obscure, make meaningful what seems irrelevant, synthesize what seems discordant. If it is bad theology, it may reach misunderstanding instead of understanding, whereas the church believes that its preaching, when it adheres to its proper object, can never arrive at anything but faith; this is what infallibility means. The same assurance cannot be extended to theology.

The reason why theology lacks this assurance is precisely that theology is the application of human learning; the preaching of the church is a charismatic office, but human learning is not and cannot be any better than its erudition and its methods. By definition it is open to error and ignorance. The human learned disciplines involved in theology have been philosophy, history, literary criticism and interpretation, textual criticism, even the study of languages. The "theologian" when he "theologizes" is always in fact doing one of these things; "theology" has no distinct method, only a distinct object. Success in philosophy, history, criticism or language is possible only by the careful application of correct methods to complete evidence. Wherever there is even a slight failure in methodology or care or the collection of evidence, error is certain to follow. It may not be a significant error, and it may easily be corrected with improved method or fuller evidence, but it is the nature of these disciplines that they proceed in this way with these risks. No scholar ever expects to produce the definitive work in philosophy, history, criticism or linguistics. It is again the nature of these disciplines that they grow; and growth in learning means not only the advance of knowledge but the abandonment of errors. Because theology is human learning, it is subject to error. Like other learned disciplines, its errors are corrected and growth ensues only by the use of its own materials and methods, not from some other agent.

This could be expanded, but it would be largely repetition and illustration; I have tried to summarize the position briefly, at the risk both of some obscurity and of some loss of persuasion. But this brief summary of what theology is suggests that it is more accurate to say that there is theology in the church than that the church theologizes. The theologian in the church operates in a private capacity. The authors of the gospel used theology in composing their narratives and discourses; they were engaged in teaching, not in proclaiming. Paul used theology, and he distinguished it from the proclamation; when he spoke of virginity or the covering of women's heads at worship, both he and his readers knew the difference between this and his proclamation of the saving death and resurrection of Jesus. If theology is a learned discipline, it will flourish best if it is carried on with that freedom which the private investigator has; it is for the church to use the material of theology to that degree to which it is useful in preaching. Officially sponsored research in the church is subject to the same dangers to which such research is subject everywhere. It is quite dishonest to claim that the officers who sponsor or discourage research are anything more than human, and that is what I mean by danger.

Having said that the church has no commission to theologize, I must add that the church has to theologize if it is to fulfill its mission of preaching. This may mean to support theology carried on with the freedom which learning demands; but without theology the church is unlikely to speak to the world in which it lives, especially to the learned world. It is unfortunate that in the modern church our officers seem to feel unable to say anything which is not official. Most of the writings of Augustine were not published as pastoral letters to the diocese of Hippo; they were the works of a private theologian speaking as such. It is now over twenty years (and the references have escaped me) since the then Archbishop of Tuam responded in an Irish theological journal to a Jesuit who had a novel theory about the interpretation of Mark 3:21. By the judicious use of the Greek dictionary His Grace proved that the Jesuit could not possibly be right. But it was the Greek dictionary, not His Grace, which gave the article its weight.

Why do not prelates engage in theological discussion? They know that if they do they must do so under the rules, which are that their positions must be supported by arguments and that they might be proved wrong. I really do believe that very few bishops are so small that they will engage in no discussion where thay cannot strike the floor with their crozier. Many of them can make genuine contributions to theology; and those who feel that they cannot might learn more about what theology is, what it can and cannot do, and why there cannot be an "authoritative" theology. We might even be spared such remarks as that of an eminent prelate, quoted to me by his priests as saying that he depended on the notes he had from his seminary days, forty-four years earlier; they were, he said, as good now as they were then. Possibly he was right, and that is frightening. If bishops were willing to be theologians, there might be less chance of theological illiterates becoming the official teachers of dioceses.

The church must theologize because it cannot answer contemporary questions without contemporary learning. It will, to use a phrase too often repeated, answer the questions of 1973 with the answers of 1873. It will hear distinguished prelates like Cardinal Ottaviani described as one of the finest minds of the eighteenth century—quoted from an unknown source, not original with me, but I agree. The need of the church for theology is best illustrated by reference to some instances when it had bad theology; and we need not mention Galileo. The Fifth Ecumenical Council serenely condemned Theodore of Mopsuestia of heresy on the basis of texts which had been falsified. Almost no statement of the official teaching agencies on biblical criticism made before 1943 is still respected and honored in the church. The syllabus of errors of Pius IX is better described as a syllabus of verities, although this exaggerates the situation; but almost every one of the propositions has become a commonplace in scholarship. The methods and manipulation of the evidence uncovered in the excavations of Peter's alleged tomb would get anyone who did this in the world of learning expelled from the lodge.

Anyone who has read the report of the committee appointed to investigate the theologians of Catholic University will recognize that my thesis is in substantial agreement with their conclusions—in fact, closer than substantial. Strange as it may seem, they seem to think that theology is safer and better if the bishops leave it alone. The report insists that the ultimate judges of the competence of a theologian are his peers. This principle is valid in every learned discipline in every civilized country; and no one has shown that theology is an exception. The theologian does not preach, he theologizes; he speaks with no authority other than his arguments. He can be controverted and refuted by anyone who has the tools and wishes to take the trouble. He has no defense except his learning but that defense should be allowed him. If he exceeds his competence and claims an authority which he lacks, he loses any claim to respect. If he suppresses or distorts the evidence, he will lose standing in the learned community. We have no comparable protection against bishops who exceed the terms of their mandate. And it does exceed the terms of the episcopal mandate to speak with authority in theology without doing the work required to make a theological statement. Everything I have said here is open to discussion, criticism and refutation; but I have a deaf spot to the thumping of croziers on the floor. They are just not theological arguments.

*Chapter Twelve*

# EASY LIVING

**T**WO STATEMENTS by Paul VI in a single week seem to me to demand a response. The two statements are summarized thus: the first is a recognition of a certain widespread mistrust toward the exercise of the hierarchical ministry. The second, is that a desire for easy living is responsible both for the opposition to *Humanae Vitae* and for the decline of vocations to the priesthood and the religious life. My response must necessarily be brief, but I hope to make it pointed; and one response can answer both statements. The response is a question: has the Holy Father considered the possibility that the widespread mistrust of the hierarchical ministry is due to the fact that the hierarchy is basically untrustworthy? If Paul VI is allowed to see some of the discussions of *Humanae Vitae,* he must recognize that not all of the discussions are written with undisciplined passion. A bit of cool reason has crept into some writings, and I know no critic of the encyclical who has fled to tears on the question. The basic reason why the encyclical is not trusted is that the encyclical imposes a rigorous obligation without equally rigorous conviction. If the Pope is not allowed to see these discussions, then his staff is untrustworthy; if he is allowed to see them, then he himself is untrustworthy.

The decline of vocations is an alarming fact, so alarming that hierarchical authorities have not yet made the figures public. A desire for soft living, I have said elsewhere, is not convincing in the United States. Our youth have shown a readiness to en-

91

roll themselves in such things as the Peace Corps, certainly a type of career which has less soft living than one can find in Roman ecclesiastical palaces. I deeply resent this imputation against our young people from prelates who notoriously like soft living. I know nothing about the personal life of Paul VI; I have seen pedestrians nearly run down in Rome by the chauffeur-driven limousines of cardinals, which proceed as if the streets were empty. I saw the papal limousine coming down the Corso one afternoon at a speed of at least forty miles an hour preceded at a rather short distance by a screaming escort of Roman motorcycle policemen. Come off it, Your Holiness. You can read lessons to no one about soft living.

Our soft living youth respond to military service in a paradoxical way. One response is accepting the service; acceptance may be misguided, but it is not soft. The other response is to reject it and to suffer public obloquy and imprisonment. This too may be misguided and is thought misguided by many, but it is not soft. I have talked to young men who know they could escape military service by entering a novitiate or a seminary. They respect the vocation too much to use it for this purpose; I do not think this is soft. I will take the Pope and the bishops seriously about the vocation crisis when they ask those who leave why they leave and those who do not come why they do not come. Failing this survey, I shall allow myself the same type of conjecture about motives which Paul VI allowed himself in his statement about soft living.

I ask his Holiness whether he has considered the possibility that young people do not think they can serve God and the church under the obedience of Paul VI and many of the bishops and religious superiors in the church now. I ask him to consider whether the quality of our hierarchical government is such as to attract candidates. Religious communities and diocesan seminaries have a traditional program which is intended to destroy personal character and personal integrity. This destruction is proposed with the highest motivation; one destroys the self to become Christ. Too often one simply destroys oneself. The actual work of clergy and religious does not justify the destruction of self. The officers of the church turn out to be the major obstacles to the work of the church, not the leaders in the mission of the church. One has destroyed oneself for an enterprise which is often as secular as any human enterprise in the world. I ask that this be considered among the possible explanations for the vocation crisis. You can tell people too long that they are nothing, have nothing, and can do nothing (Thomas a Kempis). Either they will believe you, and then they are nothing, have nothing, and can do nothing; or they will not believe you, and they will hate you for the consummate liar you are.

Let us consider whether it is not a notably desirable component of soft living to be in a position where others must do your will. Many religious priests have shared my experience, and it is a conversation piece in informal clerical gatherings. The experience is the set, prolonged and deliberate campaign of religious organizations to convince the subjects while they are young that they cannot possibly earn a gainful living, and that they would starve or freeze were it not for the bounty of their religious superiors, who furnish them with quite unearned food, clothing and shelter. I am happy to have lived long enough to attest that this is a damned lie.

Perhaps it is no more than a desire for soft living which makes one seek that basic respect for the person which hierarchical authorities consistently and habitually deny to those whom they govern. But let us at least have it analyzed. Let us measure the desire for basic respect of the person against the pathological jealousy of authority and the compulsion to impose one's will which one sees illustrated in so many prelates. Let us be sure that it is softness which makes so many refuse a life in which their leaders inquire not how they may love the subjects, but how they may use them; a life in which for most of their adult years their personal wishes are ignored or opposed, their independent judgment and original imagination are by policy suppressed and ridiculed, and their talents are patronized. Let us ask honestly whether the desire for soft living is found on only one side of the scheme. His Holiness, with

the self-pity characteristic of the hierarchy, has said that it is
not easy to rule a diocese. In dioceses like Washington, San
Antonio, Philadelphia, Los Angeles and St. Louis it is still easier
to rule a diocese than to be ruled in it. The line of bishops who
ask to be relieved of their office, and of priests who do not want
to be bishops, is not yet quite as long as the line of priests who
are ready to take on this intolerable burden.

If priests and religious were as humble and open to criticism
as Paul VI and most ecclesiastical superiors, the whole structure
would have collapsed long ago. It has never been possible for
me to refer my critical superiors to the good God, who is in-
formed about the truth of things and can rebut my critics, as
His Holiness has done in the quoted statement. Among other
differences between His Holiness and myself, it would never
occur to me to respond to criticism in this way. I think I always
fight criticism, but secretly give it a good deal of consideration.
I take it that this may make me no more Catholic than the Pope,
and I ought to be satisfied with that. I do not think it makes
me great. Criticisms of the central administration of the church,
His Holiness is quoted as saying, are not all exact, not all just,
nor always respectful and opportune. Well, criticisms of John
L. McKenzie are not all exact, not all just, nor always respectful and opportune? Perhaps some criticisms are exact, just, respectful and opportune? Which criticisms might they be? Certainly not any criticisms made or implied in this chapter, which
is written by a man who at the moment of writing is fed up to
the gullet with self-righteousness clothed in watered silk. I have
tried to be exact, just and opportune; respect, for reasons given
or implied, I was unable to manage in this effort. I refer the interested reader to earlier efforts where I attempted to maintain
respect, and for my pains got myself under a permanent injunc-
tion with no hearing in sight.

No, the subject is expected to have risen above the soft life
to the degree which allows him to accept criticism, exact or in-
exact, just or unjust, respectful or disrespectful, opportune or
inopportune, with the silence with which Jesus went to the
cross. I myself, like all priests and religious, have had all eight

of the varieties enumerated. Most of the time I remained silent, I do believe, even if the silence covered vindictiveness. We kept silent because it was orderly procedure, also because silence might protect one from more of the same later. It was and is a system which degrades both those who command and those who obey. No one can seriously assert that the hierarchical system is a means of growth in Christian holiness. It is without doubt that single element in the church which more than any other has prevented the church from achieving the fullness of Christ. It is simply true that no human being is big enough to administer wisely and virtuously the kind of authority over others which hierarchical authority claims.

Another way of doing it, fairly clear in the New Testament, has not been seriously tried or recommended in the church on anything but a local scale since the first century. Where it was tried it did not last. No one needs to explain to me why it did not last; concupiscence needs no explanation. But one does demand an explanation for repeated statements that something is the will of Jesus Christ which he said on several occasions is not his will. I refer, of course, to statements that the officers of his church should not lord it over their brethren. If the definition of "lording it" is authentically given only by the lords, then lording it has been defined before a word is spoken.

There is no doubt that the soft and easy life has been a problem in the church for centuries; no one can quarrel with this statement. But when one begins to specify the soft and easy life, to point out or insinuate where it is or where it is not, one enters on uncertain ground. Some years ago I visited a small group of priests in a foreign country who conducted a small school in an environment hostile to Catholics and Europeans. They were desperately impoverished, living in a poorly heated building and eating stuff which summoned heroism in the guest to swallow it civilly. Most of them smoked. It happened to be not long after the senile blast of Pius XII against smoking as a basic vice. When I compared these smoking missionaries with the fat cats of the Vatican, I became so furious as to be nearly inarticulate—which means my response was unprintable. Even in this more liberated age of journalism it is still unprintable, so let us drop it there. I said earlier that the Pope and the Vatican can read lessons in soft living to no one.

Let us try to put the thesis of this chapter in words so plain and unadorned that no one can possibly misquote them. I submit as a possible explanation of the vocation crisis the hypothesis that the hierarchical government of the church is so often in the hands of unworthy men that candidates are discouraged, even in areas and organizations where the leadership is Christian and competent. I submit the hypothesis that the type of obedience which the ecclesiastical vocation demands can be given to no one without entering a proximate occasion of sin. I submit that the type of prelate which we have in abundance cannot reasonably expect anyone to commit himself totally to an obedience which is proved to be selfish, tyrannical, insensitive, and basically unchristian. I submit that unwillingness to surrender totally to unworthy leadership is not a sign of love of easy living.

This hypothesis is by no means a suggestion that the government of the church be abolished. It is simply a suggestion that the church find more men worthy of hierarchical responsibility. This implies immediately that the task of finding them be committed to some other agency that the agency which has hitherto been in charge of appointments. Beyond this I am not obliged to proceed at this point. I have some faith that the church still has men in its membership who can hold hierarchical responsibility in that competent and Christian manner desiderated above. Such men will reconsider the exercise of authority, and will effectively remove from church government the pathological love of power which seems to be our most serious problem. Obviously what I think is our most serious problem is not considered such by Paul VI. I recommend it to his attention.

*Chapter Thirteen*

# ACADEMIC FREEDOM

ONE OF THE LESS known and less quoted paragraphs of the acts of the Second Vatican Council runs as follows in Abbott and Gallagher's edition of the texts. It comes at the very end of Chapter II of "The Church Today" (*Gaudium et Spes*): ". . . let it be recognized that all the faithful, clerical and lay, possess a lawful freedom of inquiry and of thought, and the freedom to express their minds humbly and courageously about those matters in which they enjoy competence." The presence of this sentence in the acts of an ecumenical council permits me to treat academic freedom as a legitimate topic for theological comment. It is tempting to set forth the theological basis of academic freedom, but space does not permit. It is tempting also to discourse on the hidden reservation placed by many on the text of the Vatican Council quoted above, which may be thus expressed: "This statement is intended in no way to limit the power of ecclesiastical authorities to do anything they damn please to inhibit freedom of inquiry, thought and expression." However, my purpose is to give some attention to some of the real threats to academic freedom which one can see in the world of the present.

The academic community is generally seen in three divisions: administration, faculty and students. Beyond the academic community proper one has interested bodies and persons such as trustees, legislatures, governors and presidents, and parents. It is evident that any or all of these together can be a threat to academic freedom, and that all of them have been at some time or another. My observations lead me to think that the greatest threat to academic freedom in recent years has come from the students, and they would not be a threat if they were not aided and abetted by enough teachers and administrators to enlarge their power.

I am going to be direct and brutal in the example I give; and I accept the risk of choosing an example of which most observers say it is impossible to ascertain the real facts of the case. I will premise that most of the difficulty of ascertaining the facts comes not from the complications of the situation—the issues are not beyond the grasp of people engaged in academic work—but from the calculated mendacity of most of the people involved in the business. I refer to the University of California at Berkeley.

The lies of the participants have so obscured reality that it is not even possible to determine accurately how seriously the university has been impeded in its mission. I have a few acquaintances who have concluded that Berkeley is no longer a university and who have therefore gone elsewhere. I can only report this as their judgment; I cannot evaluate it, and other acquaintances are sure that this judgment is in error. But the university has been impeded in its mission and it has been impeded by students or by those who posed as students. As far as one can gather, these groups contend that unless the university corrects what they consider serious defects, they will do all they can to see that the university is forced to cease operations. Behind this is an unstated proposition that the academic freedom of those who do not accept either their criticisms or their solutions of the problems cannot be defended.

In a life spent almost entirely—since the age of five—in educational institutions in one capacity or another, I have developed a fairly typical faculty attitude toward educational administrators, an attitude which is less than warm and sympathetic. Teachers feel that they know as much about the seamy side of higher education as any student, and that they can criticize administrators with a depth of material which students do not have. Yet many of us, after years of feuding with administrators, suddenly realize that when we are forced to choose between leaving the schools with administrators and surrendering to student radicals, we have to take the administrators. We are irritated because the radical students make it impossible in our generation to do anything about our own criticisms of administration. They have forced us into a united front which we detest.

At this point a reader might say that I ignore issues and concentrate on tactics. If I respond that I rejected early in life the maxim that the end justifies the means, I shall be told that the maxim has become quite respectable. I shall be challenged to dispute such questions as commitment to the military-industrial complex, the relations of the university to its neighborhood, and black studies. I will argue them, but not while someone sits in my office or shouts in my classroom; and I must confess I do not understand what is so reactionary about this attitude. As a long defender of the principle of nonviolence, I confess that I might have difficulty finding some nonviolent way of ejecting such oafs from my office or classroom, but they would surely be ejected. I want to start a new campus organization initialed SOS, which stands for "Stamp Out Slobs." I just do not see a world of peace, freedom, justice and charity emerging from a surrender to slobism.

It is annoying to have one's stand against slobism taken without further ado as full support of all that is wrong with universities, especially since many of us were talking about these wrongs before the members of SDS were born. It might be worth recalling that the ideology which permits the radical students to criticize the establishment has been mostly produced and cherished in universities, and that they would literally destroy the very institutions which feed them intellectually. A major university is a very large and complex phenomenon which cannot be judged simply on its holdings in ghetto real estate, its research commitments with defense and industry, or the number of black faculty and students or the number of courses in black studies. If one talks of tolerance of evil to radical students—or more simply, how does one talk to radical students? They listen only to each other, if to each other. Ultimately one is most offended by their self-righteousness. They have not lived long enough either to have done or to have suffered real evil.

But I wander from my point, which is academic freedom. It is true that it is the self-righteousness of the radicals which is most offensive; but it is their candid attack on academic freedom which makes them dangerous. We can stand slobs; we have to stand them because there are so many of them. But one who does not believe in academic freedom does not believe in freedom at all. Academic freedom is meaningfully defined only as the right of a scholar and teacher to express views and opinions which I reject. The existence of racism does not impose any one particular solution of the problem. It takes a dedicated liberal to maintain that academic freedom entitles a teacher and scholar to teach and defend racism; but it does. Morally, racism is less offensive to the majority than premarital sex, or at least it is on the same level, which means that it is done privately and disapproved publicly. If one believes in academic freedom and has views about racism and premarital sex, he believes that the opposing views can be effectively refuted only by rational discourse. The only antecedent fear of a racist professor is that racism seems to be by definition a denial of rational discourse. This denial ought to remove anyone from the academic community, and in my judgment it also removes most radical students.

We have had the plea that they cannot reach the establishment, and it is true that sometimes the establishment closes the channels of discourse. Students are not the only threat to academic freedom, and historically they have not been the major threat. But recent events have made the establishment much more ready to engage in discourse. To many students discourse seems to mean that they tell us what they want and we do it. This is the kind of discourse which Hitler could have accepted. The plea that "they" will not listen is no longer valid, and it never was valid across the board. It is hard to think of a more permissive administration than the distinguished group of men who administer the universities of Harvard and Chicago. When students say they can reach these men only by disrupting the operation, the disinterested observer has to conclude that the students are lying in their teeth. What they mean is that they lost the argument and are therefore entitled to wreck the plant. In our corrupt and decadent society this is not taken as proof of maturity. One who believes in rational discourses believes in the rare possibility that he might be proved wrong.

I have not touched on what has become the gut issue, which is the right of the university administration to resist aggression on its operations. I take it so obviously for granted that president, vice-president, dean or janitor may not enter my classroom or office uninvited and tell me to terminate what I am doing that I simply cannot bring myself to see why students have this right. I yield in such instances only to the fire department. To anyone else I will offer all the resistance in my power, and I mean anyone. *Life* magazine, to tell you the truth, queered student radicalism for me with its pictures of those apes in Grayson Kirk's office. What does one do when one encounters barbarians? According to my principles I should engage in rational discourse. I am ready to engage, but there are postures inept for rational discourse. Traditionally, university presidents have handled student mobs by addressing them with clear threats of expulsion. If these primitive tactics are rejected, I do not understand why anyone should forbid the president to call the police. When the objections to police or to intra-university succor are all weighed, the answer is that demonstrators will brook no interference from anyone. They want the right of aggression without resistance. Often they are crybabies.

I do not like to end this with the implication that universities become bright and clean simply by settling student disorders. The radicals have some points, and if they are ready to make them in the academic forum they will be heard, discussed and criticized. I am not sure that many of them are adult enough for the third of these, but we owe them the opportunity. There are professional societies, believe it or not, which are concerned with the quality of education. There are the vast majority of teachers, who are deeply concerned with the quality of education. We become impatient with sophomores who tell us that the worst thing about the university is the presence of Dow and CIA recruiters on the campus. About some other issues the students are not moving their little finger, nor will they, because they do not care to study or discuss the problems. The demonstration is on the intellectual level of the football rally, and about as demanding. I remarked once to some students that the things they wanted most would not be done until some odious old men sitting in a private office decide that they should be done; and they will not make this decision until they are convinced that it is the right thing to do. Odious old men of this type have spent long lives resisting irrational pressure; their attitude is that people who employ irrational pressure cannot have much to say in favor of their position. No one who has much experience in education is unaware that students have insights which their elders often miss. The quickest way to make the elder reject your insight is to try to ram it down his throat. He may have spent most of his life keeping his mind open and his throat closed, if you will pardon the metaphor. The universities need all the help they can get to be what a university ought to be, a community of learning. Help is just what radical students are denying them. I suggest they go have their revolution off campus.

*Chapter Fourteen*

# THEOLOGIAN AND CRITIC

THE PROBLEM of the role of the theologian in the church and in society is hardly new, and it will never be solved; the question is answered each time any theologian makes a decision which affects his role. These decisions scarcely ever fail to arouse adverse comment both from his fellow professionals and from laymen—laymen here meaning those who are not professional theologians. One recent writer, discussing the magisterium, observes that the statements of the Pope, while they have to be founded in research, should reflect the charismatic authority of the supreme teacher—otherwise the Pope will be just another theologian.

Well! I do not think the destiny of being "just another theologian" is likely to attract many young scholars to the discipline. On the other hand, the prospect of being just another married couple will not discourage people from marrying. It would not be hard to find men in the list of Peter's successors who could best be described as "just another Pope." Was Mr. Musial just another ball player? I think the Pope, any Pope, would be just another theologian if his theological work were mediocre; and not every Pope has risen even to the level of mediocrity. Good theology needs no bush; it is not "authoritative teaching," was never meant to be, and serves quite another function.

Or consider: If the Pope speaks in such a way that his charismatic authority does not appear, and thus becomes just another

103

theologian, does this imply that the theologian is without his own charisma? Thomas Aquinas—just another theologian—thought that the charisma of the trade was wisdom; with that insight which always keeps Thomas Aquinas from being just another theologian, he made the gift of wisdom a function of the virtue of charity. He who does not love cannot be wise. This is said without regard to the value of learning, which I am not about to discount; learning is that by which I live. It is not a charisma. Not all theologians are charismatic; neither are all Popes. We have to assume that their office puts the charisma within their reach. The learning of the theologian validates his strictly theological work; nothing but the charisma of wisdom will validate his appearance in other than a strictly professional role.

Who can claim wisdom? The truly wise man, like Socrates, is the last man to claim it. How, then, can the theologian take upon himself a role which he cannot fulfill without wisdom—for example, the role of critic or prophet? I can tell you how this happens: he sees, or thinks he sees, the necessity for saying something or doing something. He sees that he can do it. He sees that others are not doing it, whatever be their reasons. It occurs to him that perhaps he ought to do it. Unless he can bury this thought quickly and permanently, he will ultimately do it. When he does it, he realizes that he is claiming wisdom. With a sinking feeling, he sees that he may be proved a fool. It he had not spoken or acted, he would have been proved no more than a coward, and no one besides himself would have known it. The wise man, it turns out, is not proved wise until he has run the risk of folly.

Since I raised the role of prophet, let me put it down. I have to put it down because the title has occasionally been given me. My professional studies compel me to be familiar with the prophetic literature, and I can deny the title with as much assurance as I can deny anything. A colleague at a recent meeting was kind enough to deny the title after one of those present had bestowed it. Since the colleague deals with New Testament, there should have been no surprise when I invoked Mark

6:4; Matthew 13:57; Luke 4:24 as appropriate texts. But I see nothing in the role of theologian which would keep a theologian from being a prophet if he has the call. Apparently there are others who do see something; I wish they would tell me what it is. "Let him stick to his theology"—they would probably use the proper word, exegesis, if they could spell it. But let me say with Amos that I am not a prophet nor a son of a prophet; I must confess to having been a critic—and yes, Father, I took pleasure in it, sometimes with myself, sometimes with others.

May the theologian be a critic? If anyone will take the trouble to read my mail, he will know the question is silly. The proper way to rephrase the question is: May anyone be a critic? The clear and firm answer is No. Neither I nor anyone else may speak as Jesus spoke to the Pharisees because: 1) I am not Jesus; 2) there are no more Pharisees; 3) why do you not get lost, or married or something? It never occurred to me that I am Jesus, or even his vicar. It had not occurred to me that there are Pharisees, although I have sometimes thought of publishing the thesis that the Pharisees did not reject Christianity; on the contrary, they accepted it, joined the church, and were promoted to high office. It did occur to me that silence in the presence of massive injustice might be a sin. The question, of course, is whether it is massive injustice in whose presence I stand. I read somewhere that each man is responsible for a personal judgment about justice and injustice, and about love and hatred. The difference between me and most of my fellow theologians is that I was able to speak from a position of strength which they do not have for reasons which it is none of my business to know.

The critic runs the risk of being foolish and unkind. Let me assure you that he will not lack those who will tell him so, and he has to evaluate their criticisms of his criticisms. I do not want to imply that my mail is mostly hostile; on the contrary, it is by far mostly favorable. Occasionally the quality of the adverse mail reaches a level of vileness which confirms me in my criticism. I could torpedo the whole conservative wing of the church by publishing a small handful of letters. I do wonder why I am invited to get married, as if it were a curse or something. Perhaps the parents of such correspondents were not married. There is also a tendency to use the diminutive (and not as what is called a caritative!). Bishop Shannon becomes Jimmy, Charles Davis becomes Charley, Gregory Baum becomes Jewboy (forgive me, Gregory, but you probably get this in your own mail). Guilt by association, of course, should not be invoked. The fact is that I myself could in no way feel comfortable with the support of such pathological personalities, and I do feel comfortable with the hatred. Anything I say which evokes such responses cannot be all bad.

What is worse, these poor people betray a terrible insecurity with their church and their hierarchy. If I thought the church and the hierarchy were so feeble that my criticisms would weaken them, I would be terrified. On the contrary, I am sure that the Papacy and Paul VI are quite strong enough to bury critics like me; I simply wish they would make a few improvements before they do—or after, if it has to be that way. I think the authorities have done the most graceful thing they could do with my criticisms, and that is to ignore them publicly, and —so far and to my knowledge—engage in no devious counter-moves. I turn my head rather carefully at regular intervals, and it has not yet fallen off.

Ultimately the critic must make his own judgment whether he has escaped the danger of folly and unkindness. Naturally it is a great help to have the reactions of readers and listeners, and they should be both favorable and hostile; hardly anything is going to elicit only one type of response. But the reactions cannot substitute for the critic's own responsibility. He must be ready to take a position for which he has no support. It is to be assumed that such positions will be rare; in fact, it is safe to assume that it will be very hard to persuade the critic that he is under this necessity. The danger of unkindness is great. Hardly anyone has the evangelical meekness by which criticism is accepted as a favor, and if it were displayed it would make the critic uncomfortable as nothing else would. By this I imply that the unkindness is in the recipient as well as in the critic; criticism can be unkindly delivered and unkindly received. By the standards applied to some contemporary criticism, Jesus was unkind. By the same standards he should have refrained from criticism entirely. I do not believe that either the critic or his critics can ever reach a satisfactory state of mind about the criticism; and this could be enough to discourage the critic from continuing to criticize. At the risk of being unkind once more, I suspect that this is intended.

The more recent conversations and correspondence which have further obscured the role of the theologian lead to a conclusion which will surprise some. The conclusion is that the theologian-critic, and in particular this one, is a phony liberal and a paper tiger. The talkers have proved their futility; it is time for them to move over and get out of the way of the activists. I should drop the typewriter and pick up the banner. At my age I find this revolting, and I think even my juniors should understand why. During a series of demonstrations in Chicago the *Sun-Times* had some pictures of some remarkably unsexy young women from the Ladies' Auxiliary of the SDS carrying banners. It is true that they were dressed for comfort and perhaps for combat and that they had their mouths open, but the picture recalled to my mind Dr. Samuel Johnson's dictum that all cats are grey in the dark. I will not say that I would look this bad carrying a banner, but I could approach it; and I would certainly look more foolish than these *jeunes filles.*

It is indeed the truth that the writers and the talkers have had their chance and failed, and that action and only action is now imperative? Some chapters back in this book I vented a few ideas on revolution, among them the observation that the revolution devours the moderates before it devours the reactionaries. One feels confined, there is no other word for it, when he hears in the same day that he has exhibited raw anger and lack of compassion and that he is a toothless paper tiger. Retirement comes to mind, a thought which I know many will support; or why not stick to exegesis, if one's words are futile and one's physical energy is not up to demonstrating? Theology even without engaging in social criticism is a full-time job, and one cannot do one's work if one expands one's activity.

This, however, is for many an illustration of just what student radicals find wrong with universities; the professors are each wrapped up in total dedication to his field, usually with a priority of research over teaching, and detached from the urgent problems of the real world. What is asked is a change of life style and indeed a change of orientation. At a certain age this is practically impossible, and when it is demanded one is entitled to convincing arguments that it is necessary. I do not suppose that the demand for action rather than criticism is equivalent to a demand that universities as scholars and faculty as individuals renounce the pursuit of learning, but it comes close to it. I regard a world in which the pursuit of learning is not practiced as a world no better than the one we have now. The pursuit of learning, it may be alleged, does nothing to solve modern problems; I think this allegation can be made only if one is profoundly ignorant of what the pursuit of learning has been and is. There are universities which survive without supporting research; it may be significant that the activist students are not interested in attending them. This attitude toward scholarship affects all scholars, not only the scholar-critics.

Yet it would be dishonest to say that universities and scholars are never guilty of irrelevance. Perhaps the scholar exhibits the vice of being above all criticism. I do not think my juniors really wish me to engage in physical action, nor do they think —I hope—that I have become totally irrelevant. That thought will occur to those who have chosen anarchy as a way of life. I try to criticize authority, not to wreck it. Those in authority will live to regret it if they fail to notice the difference. It is called "fawning adulation" when courtiers praise the ruler for doing something which they know is mindless or cruel. Criticism hopes that the authority will strengthen itself by purging itself of its faults and does not really want the faults to be purged.

The failure of the scholars to be critics of the scene has much to do with the charge of irrelevance. If the learned community really stands for learning, it must also stand up for those social values which make it possible for a learned community to survive and be respected. If the learned community will accept its responsibility of being the conscience of society, it may protect the society from destruction by the radicals. If it proclaims peace when there is no peace, it will fall with the fallen—Jeremiah, if you are wondering who. We scholars are ambiguous before our students because they are not sure whether we are the lackeys of society. I would hope that we can make it clear both to the power structure of society and to the radicals that we ourselves are not radicals when we criticize the society for what deserves to be criticized. I have just realized, and I close with the realization, that my younger colleagues think I am a phony liberal and a paper tiger because I do not have enough company to be a force in the church.

*Chapter Fifteen*

# THE COLLAR:
# BADGE OF SERVITUDE?

**M**ORE and more priests, particularly on campuses, have adopted the customary lay garb of suit and tie. The principle governing the costume is that a teacher as such is neither clerical nor lay, and that his clerical identity has nothing to do with his teaching office. Hence his clerical indentity should not be affirmed by the clerical costume. The position seemed quite reasonable, and it has been widely followed. The Archbishop of St. Louis expressed his disapproval, but I have the feeling that I am old enough to decide what I wear without asking his approval. He does not ask mine. The principle is that when one is not functioning as a priest one should not dress like one.

It is interesting that one correspondent referred to the traditional clerical costume of the Roman collar. Obviously this correspondent has not seen many of the pictures of American priests before the Civil War, who wore the stocks, scarves and other varieties of neckwear worn by nineteenth century gentlemen. The Roman collar was not introduced until the latter part of the century, and it is "Roman"; it distinguished the priest from the Protestant minister. The black broadcloth suit was worn by any American male of the same period who was "dressed up"; has anyone ever seen a picture of Abraham Lincoln wearing anything else? "Traditional" is an overcharged

word in Catholicism anyway, but when one feeds me tradition
I would like it to be a little more than a hundred years old.

So why do some Catholics find it offensive when the priest
wears "lay" clothing? It may have been good enough for Peter
and Paul, but it is not good enough for me. The things I lack
which make me a lesser priest and a lesser man than Peter and
Paul are not supplied by turning my collar around. It is not the
costume, but the role which is in question; and the role means
that I must be explicitly and constantly different from the layman. It is not a need for identification; if there is a sudden emer-
gency call for a priest, no one looks around for a Roman collar.
We have to ask why some, including bishops, priests and laity,
have a fear that the priest may not be instantly recognized by
his costume.

Well, let us have some obvious examples. The costume will
keep the priest out of brothels. I hope something else besides
the collar will keep him out. It will keep him out of some forms
of entertainment such as the lower type bars, nude movies and
burlesque shows. It will not, in this country, prevent his attendance at the theatre, the opera, and sporting spectacles. Good
restaurants would rather have me with the collar than without
it; they think the collar adds class. I will add that it often gets
one seated more quickly, perhaps at the cost of a bit of anticlericalism here and there. I suspect that many really think of
the collar as a form of moral restraint on priests; and the fear
that a priest replaces the collar with lay garb for no good purpose bespeaks very little esteem for the moral firmness of priests
in general.

The collar can also be a sign of privilege, and where it is, it
is the lowest degree of ecclesiastical pomp. This varies from
place to place. It is certainly an advantage in New York,
Chicago, Philadelphia, Boston, and San Francisco. It is, in my
experience, less of an advantage in Los Angeles, Washington,
Detroit, Miami and—strangely enough—New Orleans. The
fact is—it must be confessed—that priests in the cities mentioned first have the reputation of generous spenders. A certain
caution in the way I live does not allow me to attest where the

collar is an advantage in beating traffic laws, even laws governing moving violations; I hear of a number of cities. I can attest that in Berkeley I knew a priest who was given a parking ticket by one of his own parishioners; in Berkeley the collar does not hurt, but neither does it help. As a sign of ecclesiastical pomp I do not want it, and I am not going to take the trouble to explain why. I prefer to deal with ticket sellers, head waiters, policemen, etc. as an ordinary citizen and not as a member of a privileged class.

There are no doubt places where the collar evokes hostility, but the number is diminishing and they are mostly quite remote. It is over twenty years since some priest friends told me of the palpable hostility which a priest encountered in Dallas. Big D has become much more cosmopolitan. The collar there is not what it is in Chicago, but there are not many places where it is. The collar did not keep Reeb and Morrisroe from getting shot in Alabama because they were not wearing it at the time. I doubt that it would have helped. Perhaps the only instance of its use as meaningful identification occurred in the civil rights marches of the 60's. Some Protestant colleagues admitted, with blushes, that they got out black suits and Roman collars they had not worn for years in order to have some identification for a civil rights march. Their only identification was the identification of a Roman Catholic priest. On the other hand, why should one not march as a person? Many Catholics, including some bishops, felt the same way about Roman collars in civil rights marches as they felt about my wearing a necktie on a television show. They would put the civil rights in the same class with the burlesque show as far as costume is concerned. Priests should not march, and if they do they ought not to identify themselves as priests.

Perhaps enough of the sheer irrationality of the attitude is beginning to emerge so that one will wonder less why I prefer my conservative suit and tie. I may add by parenthesis that I have some sport shirts that will hit your eye from a half mile away. But I have not yet touched on the basic symbolism of clerical garb; this is, quite simply, that the wearer is not his own man, that he is somebody's property. Perhaps the military uniform has the same effect; but I have never heard the military who wear mufti on occasions criticized for abandoning their traditional garb. I do not even know the rules, except that if a military man is captured in war without a uniform he may be summarily shot according to the laws of war. I read once that 60% of American men wear some kind of uniform at work; the principle is simply this, that they wear it at work. To my knowledge, the only uniform which has the same implication of servitude as the clerical garb is the uniform of the prisoner. When the prisoner changes it, it is to escape.

I may indeed have to explain why I reject this or any other badge of servitude. I can ask why or how the priesthood ever became identified with a state of servitude, and I do not mean that servitude which is the service of the servants of Christ. To this service the clerical garb contributes nothing, and in addition it establishes an unwanted and useless gulf between the priests and the servants of Christ. Whatever he may do for them, he may not share their life and their experience. No, the servitude implied is simply the servitude of men who have very few decisions of their own in the ideal state symbolized by the costume. I do not pretend that every person is a completely free and responsible agent; but our society gives adults freedom and responsibility which the "traditional" church denies to priests. It is time that we have a clear statement of what good purpose is served by the denial.

The isolation of the priest from the laity can be observed in more than one European country. Italy is a splendid example because it is the European country to which Catholics are most likely to go first when they have the opportunity. If they have the time, they might study the proportions in which anticlericalism matches the isolation of the clergy. One hesitates to call the Italian clergy a privileged class; their standard of living is notably lower than the standards of American clergy. They have their own peculiar privileges, but we do not find them attractive. Their place is the sacristy, and this is the beginning of anticlericalism. I do not believe we have anything to learn from the Italian way; and the very fact that the collar is "Roman" ought to be a warning to us to get rid of it. We have to understand that clerical garb and clerical isolation are promoted by Italian prelates who, for inexplicable reasons, believe that the Italian pattern is ideal and should be imposed on the entire church.

On the other hand, the worker priests of France made a deliberate effort to close the gap between clergy and laity entirely. Unfortunately, the program was not allowed to endure long enough to permit a judgment of its success. "Excesses" appeared, and frightened prelates fled back to the security of clerical isolation. This assumption that there are no "excesses" associated with clerical isolation is altogether invalid; but perhaps I do the prelates an injustice in thinking they made such an assumption. It may very well be that they prefer the excesses of clerical isolation to the excesses of clerical association with the laity. It is hardly a secret that many prelates prefer concubinage to marriage of priests. One must realize that celibacy is defined as the unmarried state, not as a state of chastity. If anyone finds this moral cynicism revolting, he will get no quarrel from me.

Archaism is never a sign of vitality, and it is usually a sign of approaching dissolution. Hence one hesitates to suggest a return to the church of the New Testament. I do not make such a suggestion, but let us notice a few things. Nothing in the New Testament indicates that there was any difference in dress, status, manner of life and such things between the apostle (and elder or deacon) and other members of the apostolic churches. There was not even clerical celibacy to distinguish the clergy; the option which Paul offered to Christians (I Corinthians 7:7-9, 25-38) permitted greater freedom of choice than the most recent pontifical declarations on the subject permit. These declarations do not face the nagging problems of the isolation of the clergy. Is it a good thing? Does it further the mission of the church? I do not mean to identify celibacy with clerical isolation, although the abandonment of compulsory celibacy would do more than any other single factor to take the clergy out of isolation. The writers of the New Testament books spoke to men in a world which the writers knew and experienced as fully as those to whom they spoke. The modern priest does not have this community with those to whom he must speak. I have to state my personal conviction that this is a net loss, and that it is one of the more important factors to be considered when we think about our crisis of relevance.

We are all aware of what appear to be extravagant efforts to identify with the laity. Some of us are amused at the nun in miniskirt, others are angry; personally I think a miniskirt does no more for the nun than it does for her secular sister. The success of the miniskirt depends on the wearer. For years we have had the athletic red-blooded young priest who won his way to the heart of young people by having a good fast ball or knowing his way around popular music. They often looked more like scoutmasters than clergy, a doubtful gain. But where isolation is a way of life there is no easy and natural way to break out of it; any effort is likely to be clumsy. Any effort, clumsy or not, will be resented by those who want the priest to remain a slave, a symbol, a kept man, a perpetual adolescent. If most priests began to speak as responsible adults, they could endanger the power structure; they might even say something Christian. Now the Groppis and the Berrigans are oddballs, and we are happy as long as we can be sure of it. Suppose they were typical; God spare us!

Ultimately the easiest way to reach people is to join them. I wrote somewhere that priests are really at ease only in the company of other priests; when they are with prelates or with laymen, they feel they are under surveillance. Well, folks, stop watching and we will both be more comfortable. When I was much younger in the priesthood, I was extremely conscious of the stares which the clerical costume elicited. As one gets older one ceases to notice them. But if anyone stares at my ties from Lytton's, I know it is my taste and not my beliefs and morals which are attracting interest. I found the best way to handle the stares was to stare right back; but even then I wondered why the work of God should engage one in a duel of stares. Give the collar back to the Romans.

*Chapter Sixteen*

# THE METHOD OF "INSIGHT"

INVITATIONS to learned conferences are frequent enough in the life of a professor to give him some choice of accepting and refusing. But an invitation to a learned conference in Florida during Easter Week with an opportunity to rest for a few days before Easter is the kind of invitation which one is likely to accept and then ask what the topic of discussion is to be. Such a conference was held at St. Leo's College a while back, and the topic of discussion was the theological method of Father Bernard Lonergan, mostly as set forth in *Insight*. The personnel of the conference was of a character which made name-dropping routine. The atmosphere was casual and the weather was kindly. The organization of the conference was as good as I have seen, and far better than most. The participants were required to earn their dinner by preparing a substantial paper. These were multiplied and distributed before the conference began, and thus the time of the conference was devoted to discussion. The eighty or so scholars in attendance are all quite well known for their fluency, and the discussions did not lag; rather at times they became diffuse. But they dealt with matters of theological importance; and we believed that even in the confusion of 1970 some theological clarity was worth the searching. I am not sure we found it, but we may have gone some way toward identifying the confusion. The papers are now published, and they make a sizable book.

Lonergan is the theologian's theologian, and I dare say many who read this will say "Who?" in an astonished tone when they hear of a conference held on the work of one man. In the trade, *Insight* is regarded as the most important work on the method of speculative or systematic theology to be written in over a hundred years. The reader may indeed wonder what speculative or systematic theology is; and he must recognize that this is the type of theology which produces doctrinal formulations. Some of these formulations become the official teaching of the church; whether they do become official or not, they become the generally accepted ways of stating Catholic belief.

That speculative theology can be important outside the circle of professional theologians can be seen by referring to the condemnation of Galileo and the near condemnation of evolution in the nineteenth century. Both of these misadventures were due to faulty theological method more than to anything else. They were not simply due to misinformation. Sound method does not provide information, but it prevents one from making firm statements when information is lacking. It furnishes a method of self-criticism. No method for this can be perfect and always effective, but it seems—at the risk of hindsight—that it should protect theology against blunders about the solar system and evolutionary process. We can see that these blunders were committed because theologians thought that they need not consult the natural sciences in order to answer the pertinent questions. This is bad method now, and it was bad in earlier centuries.

Speculative theology is still living off the endowment of Thomas Aquinas. Aquinas transformed theology in the thirteenth century by making it speak in the categories of the philosophy of Aristotle. Since Aquinas did not know Aristotle in the original Greek and since the translations which he used were in many respects quite imperfect, his philosophy was more independent of Aristotle than he realized. No theologian since has matched massive genius with self-confidence as Aquinas did. The method vindicated itself almost immediately, although it should not be forgotten that many thought at the time that Aquinas was a dangerous innovator. As a matter of fact he was, and there have been constant efforts to see that he was the last of this kind.

The philosophy of Aristotle as modified by Aquinas presented a world view. No one before Aquinas except Origen had attempted to locate theology in a world view; and the hostility engendered by Origen's effort was so great that many of his works have perished. In the thirteenth century it was the most comprehensive and rational world view which had been offered, and it was successful largely because there was no competition. Aquinas was willing to engage in dialogue with the primitive natural sciences of his time and even to write about them. Understanding the world, he thought, was a path to the understanding of God, and no area of knowledge was foreign to the theological enterprise.

The system had its weaknesses. The natural sciences were, as I have said, primitive; we praise Aquinas for his interest in the sciences rather than for his knowledge of them. Historical method and historical criticism were unknown in medieval learning, and they are unknown in the theological method of Thomas Aquinas; his successors have inherited this blind spot, and it was my own major criticism of the work of Lonergan. Too much confidence was placed in sheer dialectics, the skill of reasoning from general ideas; reliance on this skill sometimes suggests that it is unnecessary to seek particular information. The seeming power of animals to calculate is due to their possession of *vis aestimativa,* which in translation turns out to be the power to calculate. But the weaknesses were inherent in the culture in which the method was developed. We do not criticize Aquinas for not being Isaac Newton. I do not believe that theologians have been entirely faithful to the principles and methods of Aquinas when they treat them as terminal. As I understand the principles and methods of Aquinas, they were intended to leave room for more of the same kind of development which he instituted. His readers do not always know how daring some of his conclusions were when they were first proposed.

So much for the importance of theological method; it seems wise to justify bringing eighty scholars together, and in fairness it should be added that once we got started the schedule was grim. Lonergan is not another Aquinas, and he is far too intelligent to think of trying to be. No longer can a theologian hope to master even the whole of theology, much less the whole of learning. But what Lonergan can think of is the world view. To ignore the philosophy which has occurred since Aquinas is as bad as it would be to ignore the science. But there is no one system such as the Aristotelian system which one can choose for his world view; and no one has synthesized modern philosophy. Lonergan is too intelligent also for this; nor does he really pretend that he is elaborating a world view. The title of his book, *Insight*, does designate its object. He believes that philosophical understanding begins with the understanding of the act of understanding. From this philosophical achievement one may be able to move to the construction of a world view.

Naturally such a work is anthropocentric; and the reaction of some readers is hostile. Instead of the study of God—which is one translation of "theology"—Lonergan proceeds to the study of man, and not even of the whole man; he institutes a study of the mind. If Lonergan thinks that theological method cannot be analyzed unless thought itself is analyzed first, he is not saying anything absurd. It is just in the areas of philosophical and scientific method that the world of thought has changed since Thomas Aquinas. As a theologian I have spent considerable time in my life with theological literature, and I can attest that theologians better than anyone else succeed in not being men of their times when they deal with theology. They sometimes exhibit the weaknesses of the method of Aquinas to a degree to which he never exhibited them. A revolution in theological method must begin by catching up with the world of thought; otherwise we might as well stay with Aquinas. Lonergan is remarkably well equipped to do this.

One need not have much acquaintance with the world of modern thought to know that modern philosophy and science is humanistic at best, atheistic at worst, and generally unfriendly to the theological enterprise. I believe most modern philosophers and scientists group theology with alchemy and astrology in the republic of learning. The refusal of theology to engage in dialogue with the sciences since Galileo has more than a little to do with this. The Christian churches, with the Roman Catholic Church in the front ranks, have spent much of the last hundred and fifty years resisting the progress of scientific learning. Theologians have no right to be surprised that philosophers and scientists are hostile; theologians have done everything they can to elicit hostility. In this generation theological imperialism has become very feeble, and it is rarely met outside of Rome; but we still have enough theologians and prelates who think the mission to teach includes the divine right to judge scientific problems without studying them. Lonergan's method leaves no room for this.

Whether Lonergan succeeds or not in finding a new method, it seems sure that he will shake up the theological world enough to make it aware of its problems. Theology cannot engage in dialogue with modern thought because it does not know the language. Lonergan's methodology insists that theologians must learn the language. If they do, there is some hope that modern thought will listen and understand. If we do not learn the language, we are nothing but mandarins. I hardly need to argue the point that theology has little or nothing to say about almost every problem which is urgent in the contemporary world. If we do speak, what we say is largely unintelligible.

Those who worry about the secular humanism and atheism of much of modern thought ought to remember that Aristotle was not as Thomas Aquinas made him out to be. I can get a dispute going with Aristotelians about this, but I believe the proper name for Aristotle's metaphysics is atheism and for his ethics, secular humanism. Possibly Thomas Aquinas incorporated more of Aristotle into his synthesis than a Christian synthesis could assimilate. But Aquinas was not attempting to create a systematic theology which he could present to a secular and atheistic world. Odd as it may seem, he was only trying to organize theology into a system which could be taught and learned. This modest objective is not beneath the attention of modern theologians. There is no reason to refuse the risk of learning from the humanists and the atheists; Thomas Aquinas was not afraid to take the risk.

It is now more than a few years since a bright young seminarian wrote a brief commentary on the unphilosophical character of biblical studies, as best exemplified in my writings. The young man was named Michael Novak, and I did not know that he had such a future in learning. I am glad that I answered him with courtesy and respect. He touched at the time on my own thoughts on the present and the future of theology; and the thoughts were generally that the structure of theology was shattered beyond repair. We could and did work on particular questions, but the interrelation of the separate enterprises lay out of perception. I had stopped thinking of the relevance of any biblical work to systematic theology, not because I was hostile to systematic theology but because there was no system to which I could be relevant. I thought then and I think now that this is not a healthy condition of theology. But I disclaimed any responsibility to create a philosophical synthesis, and I did not accept the affirmation implicit in his title that there is a philosophy implicit in biblical studies. I do not think that this lack strengthens biblical studies. It is implicit in biblical studies that one must admit pluralism and historical relativism in examining the Bible, and these terms are so redolent of the heresy of Modernism that we have always been careful in using them. Now they are a part of modern thought; I am not sure Lonergan's method leaves enough room for them. On the other hand, Lonergan is far from the flat and uncompromising refusal of most systematic theologians to admit the reality of history. He may leave little room for it, but his predecessors left no room.

I was invited to be a critical respondent in the conference, and my criticism was that Lonergan's method has taken little account of biblical interpretation. The criticism was not regarded as unfair; nor did I intend it to be a complete description of Lonergan's method, which is far too massive and far too carefully done to suffer from a single criticism. And even if it were to suffer from a dozen or a hundred such criticisms, it would still have values of stimulation—heuristic, Lonergan would call them—which few writers possess; one finds the same charisma in Teilhard de Chardin. Lonergan's method will almost surely not fructify finally in the form in which he has proposed it. And since he is not only aware but responsive to criticism of his treatment of history and exegesis, I expect that his complete work will at least found a synthesis of systematic theology and biblical interpretation which will be entirely new and original.

Why do I burden my readers with a report of one of the most recondite theological conversations held in the last few hundred years? Because theology is important to them whether they know it or not, and it is important that it be vigorous. We may not know what is lacking in our diet, and we may never blame the diet if our teeth fall out; but if one does not notice that his teeth are falling out he has problems that diet will not cure. Modern theology has lost its teeth and its bite. Lonergan thinks it can recover its teeth if it learns to understand modern thought and to express itself in the language of modern thought. He has written a very dense work on the methods of modern thought which he regards as the first of two volumes. The next volume, recently finished, will apply this more precisely to theology. Whether theologians adopt the method or not, the conversations which follow it will go a long way toward restoring life to speculative theology. If "life" seems too strong a word, then let us be satisfied with hoping that speculative theology will become articulate. If it does not, the church itself may have an even more serious problem with its articulation. Right now it is just not being heard.

*Chapter Seventeen*

# PROTESTERS DENIED BAIL

I WOULD LIKE to draw attention to a recent theological phenomenon—at least reductively theological. I have in mind the words uttered by two judges, I believe, in pronouncing sentence on some persons, mostly clergy and religious, who were convicted of destroying draft records. My attention wanders to the denial of bail on the grounds that these people are too dangerous to be allowed to roam at liberty until they begin to serve their sentence. The bail which was denied the protesters is normally granted to criminals convicted of such high jinks as rape, armed robbery, assault and burglary; this has been noticed by several journalists. One can be as sure as it is possible to be in predicting human behavior that the convicted protesters will not commit murder, assault, rape, mayhem or robbery if they are released on bail; the only probability is that they may destroy some draft records, for they are obviously unrepentant. I am compelled to conclude that the eminent justices who sentenced them believe that burning draft records is a more serious threat to the fabric of our society than the aforementioned types of antisocial conduct.

In the Roman Empire, Christians were charged with *odium generis humani,* which I translate roughly as hatred of people. This was not a legal charge but an expression of popular prejudice; and the prejudice went on to expand itself with the assurance that if Christians hated people, there was no crime which they were above committing. Hence any rumor about

125

the immorality of Christians was credible. In fact the Roman Christians were a meek and retiring sheep-like crowd, about as dangerous as frightened rabbits. Nevertheless they were dangerous to the Roman establishment in their own nonviolent way. The late Martin Dibelius credited a very few Christians and a very few Romans, among whom he included the emperor Decius, with the perception that Christianity would destroy the Roman Empire if it grew. It would not destroy the Empire by violence but by its moral position, which was in total opposition to all the things by which the Roman Empire sustained itself. Christianity was ultimately able to adjust its moral position to the Roman Empire when the Empire became Christian and the church became Roman, but Decius was basically right. The Roman power structure did not survive Christianity.

I may flatter the justices when I credit them with a similar perception. They believe that the republic can survive murderers, rapists, robbers and assorted thugs, who are really not a serious threat to our institutions and to public order. They believe it can survive the Mafia—which I now read is a chimaera, a nonexistent phantom created by anti-Italian prejudice. The republic can survive crime, organized and unorganized, as long as the game of crime is played according to certain rules quite well-known to criminals, police, attorneys and judges. Criminals do not attack the system, for they depend on the system for their income and their support. Crime is a major industry from which millions of people profit directly and indirectly. As yet Mr. Nader has not found it worthy of his attention; is it because Mr. Nader thinks that organized crime is less of a threat to the republic than General Motors? There will always be crime; and I hesitate to impute to the honorable justices an acceptance of the principle that if you cannot lick it, you might as well join it. Some public officials have had this principle proved on them. But the record burners flout every rule, written and unwritten. They are unpredictable, they seek no visible gain, they neither buy nor can they be bought. The republic can live with Al Capone—to pick a name I think is safe; it is endangered by obstinate men and women of principle. Capone could get bail, but the Chicago Seven could not. Capone never questioned the rights of government; he was reasonably sure that he could buy its agents off from asserting its rights. His mistake was in thinking that he could buy off the entire public; and even then who knows whether he might not have bought it if he had been willing to pay the price? The American public has never proved that it is incorruptible; and it has often been unsympathetic to the occasional incorruptible men who by accident or political necessity are elected to public office. The American public does not understand incorruptibility, and it does not understand the record burners. In the public mind they approach *odium generis humani.* Your neighborhood purse-snatcher is a victim of society, to be treated like a sick child; your neighborhood record burner attacks something we hold dear.

The justices are correct in believing that the record burners are more dangerous to the republic than robbers and burglars. The record burners meet the republic on the ground of morality. They do precisely what criminals do not do, and that is to challenge the moral authority of the republic. Criminals are not interested in the moral authority of the republic, but only in the republic's power of coercion. They do not believe in moral authority, and therefore they do not challenge it. The record burners do believe in moral authority, and they deny that the republic has it in the cases in question. One wonders whether the officers of the republic believe in moral authority, since they seem more at home with those who do not believe in it; but they do not allow anyone to interpose moral authority as a challenge to their power of coercion. They can see that moral authority, if it were accepted by enough people, could pose a serious challenge to their power of coercion.

The record burners challenge the republic precisely at that point where the republic permits no challenge. Whatever moral sovereignty a nation can gather is assembled for the purpose of war. War is the supreme effort of a state, and it makes the supreme demand on its citizens. The right to make war at that time and in that place and in that manner which public authority decides is, in the mind of those who hold public authority, the right to survive. To question the time or the place or the manner is to question the right to survive; the state cannot permit this question. It can tolerate no moral assessment of its actions, for it cannot tolerate the hypothesis of nonsurvival. Public authority must be the supreme and only judge of the morality of its actions when it engages in war. To hamper the effort of war in any way has long been judged treasonable. Criminals are not treasonable, and the difference ought to be obvious.

The difference between the attitude of the republic toward war and the attitude adopted by the Assyrian and the Roman Empires may not be perceptible; the reason it is not perceptible is that there is no difference. Our cherished freedoms do not include the freedom to question what our republic does in its own defense. The Romans said that the safety of the people is the supreme law; our distinguished judges accept this maxim, and they do seem to imply that crime is not a threat to the safety of the people. In the sense in which the adage is understood in law, crime is not a threat to the safety of the people, because the people in a general way accept crime. It is, I have said, one of our major industries. So is war. The safety of other people is not our concern. I said that the record burners attack something which we hold dear, and it is now time to identify what this cherished object is; it is our unlimited right to kill those whom we regard as our enemies when, where and in what manner it pleases us to kill them.

Certainly someone is ready to ask whether I defend the invasion of government offices and the destruction of government property. I do not defend it, and after more than a little thought upon the subject I still cannot bring myself to share even by approval in the burning of the records. In old-fashioned moral theology there were things such as contraceptive devices which were labeled "intrinsically evil." The old-fashioned moral theologians would not permit one to destroy intrinsically evil devices if they were the property of another; the theologians may have been too attached to property, and they were the same theologians who believed that there could be a just war. Nevertheless I think they were right, because in this instance they would not permit one to invade another's area of decision. The record burners may have done to the government what the government does to its citizens. If they did just that, then their offense may be so great that they should not get bail. But since they manifestly cannot do what the government does, the government gives unwitting testimony to their moral stature by denying them bail.

What I defend is the right of the citizen to dissociate himself from the crimes which his government commits in his name, allegedly in his defense, with his money. It should be a conceivable act of loyalty for a citizen to attempt to keep his government on a moral level above that of Adolf Hitler, where a cartoonist as patriotic as Bill Mauldin put us after My Lai. My friends who are record burners or who consort with record burners twit us with our ineffectiveness. I am reached by this twitting, but I really have not been impressed with the effectiveness of record burning. Yet is it so ineffective? I believe my memory serves me correctly when I recall that the FBI detachment sent to apprehend Philip Berrigan was almost twice as numerous as the detachment which was sent to entrap John Dillinger at the Biograph Theatre. Phil should be flattered at the attention, and the FBI looks utterly ridiculous. With that kind of police work no wonder we have political assassinations; it is surprising that we do not have more.

Those of us who adhere to peaceful protest, whatever that may be, are embarrassed that the government does not hate us; we simply do not annoy it enough to cause it worry. We are on good terms with the establishment, much as the Mafia is on good terms with it, because we play according to the rules. The government realizes that some of us are troubled and must speak if we can. It shows its tolerance and its championship of freedom by allowing us to speak, because it is sure that we have altogether no influence on public opinion or public policy. Should we ever have any influence, I doubt that tolerance would be continued. The rules of this game are that we do not influence public opinion or public policy. I am not thinking of anything so crude as jail; but it is altogether in character with our

American liberties that universities and foundations which become centers of peace movements and studies should hear mutters about tax exemptions. We could hardly ask for a clearer statement that our government does not allow war and peace to be treated as moral issues. In this respect it deals with war and peace as it deals with crime, which likewise is not a moral issue.

The student of Christianity wonders whether there is not something wrong with the church when it bothers the civil authority as little as we do. The history of church and state is more frequently a history of strife than a history of concord, and not always because the church was right and the state was wrong. But it is not a history of which the believer need be entirely ashamed. Whether we are adding a chapter which later generations can honor I do not know. They may judge us to be as tame a group of Christians as ever danced to any emperor's pipe. I cannot think of any crusade ever blessed by the church which has not become one of the disgraces of the church. That this crusade is different has not yet appeared.

On the other hand, we may annoy the establishment more than we know. The denial of bail to the record burners, taken together with the high probability that they will get no reduction in time for good behavior, suggests a vindictiveness which goes beyond these few individuals. That they are made "examples" in the traditional sense is clear. Possibly they must bear some of the burden of those who do annoy the government but have done nothing actionable. Should this be true, we owe them a profound apology, whatever be our judgment of the tactics they employed. Had they represented a kooky minority, it seems unlikely that the civil authorities would have shown a fear of them which it does not show of professional gunmen. They need not inspire us to burn records, but they should inspire us to do something more than flap our hands. What that might be, of course we flap our hands trying to figure out. I have noticed that attorneys often like to have portraits of famous jurists on the walls of their offices. If I can be directed to a couple of portraits of England's celebrated hanging judge, Justice Jeffreys, I can put them on my Christmas list.

*Chapter Eighteen*

# POLYGAMY

THIS IS WRITTEN after a forty-day tour of Tanzania, Uganda and Kenya, in the course of which I gave lecture series at eight different centers. This is not mentioned in order to vindicate me as an expert on Africa; we have seen too many of these forty-day wonders to have any desire to add one more to their number. My purpose is to explain how I came to encounter a theological problem which has been totally inactive in my own life in the ministry, and I suspect in the life of all those who have shared my experience in the seminary and in the ministry. They, like me, met polygamy in ethics and moral theology as a purely historical and theoretical question. We learned that the polygamy of David and Solomon and the patriarchs, apparently mentioned with approval in the Bible—for these stalwarts were Old Testament saints—was practiced by a divine dispensation. Subsequent studies in exegesis disclosed no such dispensation; the dispensation had to be presumed in order to justify the holiness of these Old Testament saints, a holiness which would be seriously imperiled by their violation of a secondary precept of the natural law. For the further development of the thesis went like so: polygamy, it was argued, was contrary to the primary end of marriage, the procreation and education of children. This argument, however, could not establish the prohibition of polygamy as a primary precept of the natural law, for the primary precepts of the natural law are not dispensable even by God Almighty; and we cannot have established saints living in contradiction to the primary precepts of the natural law. It all hangs together, and it is all obviously contrived. Most of us were ready to leave it there, since the probability of encountering a live practicing polygamist was minimal.

The few of us who went on to the study of exegesis soon became aware that the traditional statement involved some very bad exegesis. Not only is there no dispensation of polygamy for the patriarchs and kings, there is no express repudiation of polygamy anywhere in the Bible. Furthermore, all the evil consequences of polygamy, the evidence by which it was argued that polygamy is contrary to the primary end of marriage, can be observed in the polygamous households of Abraham, Jacob, David and Solomon. The first conclusion of the young exegete is that the Old Testament saints practiced polygamy because they knew no better; this saves their conscience at the cost of their moral insight. But if the young exegete becomes, as many young exegetes must, an amateur student of society and culture, he begins to wonder whether the moral insight of the Old Testament saints was as dim as he had judged it to be.

Sooner or later the student of the Old Testament is driven to investigate the structures of tribal society. Ancient Israel was indeed advanced beyond the level of tribal society, but in many ways Israel retained certain tribal customs and structures even after it had arrived at an urban-agricultural economy. Israel remembered its prehistoric ancestors as tribes, even though it is now reasonably well established that the origins of Israel were more complex than they knew. The tribe is a kinship group; this means that it is a family rather than a political society. Kinship is the basis both of the support which the members expect from the tribe and of the obligations which the tribe lays upon the members. Civilized man would find that the tribe denies him the opportunities of personal freedom and personal fulfillment which he has learned to expect. The tribesman would find that civilized society fails to furnish him with the security which the tribe gives him. Tribal society knows no depressed classes, no poor and helpless; the family does not permit any of its members to be destitute while others live with abundance. The student of society makes no value judgment at this point. The study of social structures does not disclose which structure offers its members a greater degree of basic human contentment.

The student of social structures does learn that the tribe is unable to withstand the encounter with civilization. The kinship group does not survive in political society unless it becomes isolated from the civilized community. No civilization attacks tribal society with such deadly success as European civilization, which manifests an aggressive vigor not matched by any earlier civilization. What first attracts tribesmen are the gadgets of civilization; they learn soon that it is not possible to enjoy rifles without accepting the culture which makes rifles and ammunition. Yet while civilizations rise and fall, tribal society remains to occupy the territory which civilization occupied before its collapse. The tribe outlives civilization because of its conservatism, its tenacity in retaining a way of life which experience validates as adapted to the environment. But if the environment changes, the tribe is doomed unless it moves or accepts civilization.

This lengthy background is necessary to show that tribal culture, like civilization, is a package, not merely a collection of unrelated practices. It is true that most cultures are in a state of movement rather than repose, and that movement may be either a movement toward growth or toward dissolution. But the very conservatism of tribal culture makes it less flexible than civilization. Civilization is a product of the demonic in man which drives him toward adventure and the search of the unknown; tribal culture is precisely a refusal to venture into the unknown. Tribal culture is so simple that to tamper with it may be to destroy it.

Quite apart from any travel to Africa foreseen or intended, I reached the conclusion some years ago that polygamy is a cultural problem, not a moral problem; that polygamy, far from being repugnant to the natural law in a tribal society, may indeed be demanded by the natural law in a tribal society, for reasons which I shall present immediately. The ethics of the natural law have been produced by thinkers who had no knowledge or experience of tribal society. They assumed that natural man is civilized man—and in modern times this has meant European man. Tribal man could not extablish the "nature" of man; one would as readily consider the anthropoid ape as a specimen of "human nature." I would not expect ethical thinkers to visit tribes, much less to live with them; but they might have read a book on the subject before excluding what constitutes a great part of mankind from their consideration of "human nature."

The basic reason for polygamy in tribal society is, as I have said, that tribal society is a familial society and not a political society. In a family, woman has no place except as daughter or wife, and tribal society has no place for the unattached woman. The security of woman rests on her dependence—one may say ownership—on the man who is the head of the house. Inquiry has revealed to me no explanation of the fact that in tribal society more females than males survive to adulthood. Some would see in this a confirmation of the well-known suspicion that women are the tougher, not the gentler sex. Tribes have always believed that a woman should be one of several wives rather than a superannuated daughter; for the tribesman and the tribeswoman believe that the supreme fulfillment of woman lies in bearing tribesmen. For those who have been trained in the principle that the primary end of marriage is the procreation and education of children—a tribal understanding of marriage, by the way—this belief of the tribes should not be difficult to understand.

It is no secret that the breakup of polygamous households demanded of converts by missionaries has sometimes resulted in cruelty. In particular, the expelled wives have sometimes been unable to support themselves and their children except by prostitution. One wonders whether or not missionaries have found prostitution, which is a European cultural practice, more tolerable than polygamy, which is not European. Failure to study tribal society has kept European theologians from seeing that polygamy is a commitment, not mere "lust"—the favorite curial word whenever anything concerning sex comes up for discussion. Polygamy is marriage, not concubinage; and it ought to be noticed that the rigorous Catholic teaching on perpetual monogamy has always had an extensive background of concubinage as well as of prostitution. The only household known to the tribes has been hastily wrecked, and the results, as I have observed, are cruel. One has one's doubts whether a cruel enforcement of morality has a certain claim to be Christian.

It is a cultural fact that civilization and not religion has eliminated polygamy. The polygamy of the early books of the Old Testament does not appear in the later books. The Hellenistic-Roman world was not polygamous; it certainly was not Christian, and many students doubt whether it can be called moral. In the course of time polygamy will disappear as Africa becomes entirely civilized. To say that we ought to wait for this to happen is to treat people who are living now as stepping stones toward the religion and culture of the future. I believe they have the same rights to hear the gospel as people of the future. If there is a cultural obstacle, we ought to be very sure that it is an obstacle.

St. Paul devoted much of his life and much of his correspondence to disputing those who believed that one had to become a Jew before one could become a Christian. Paul won that battle; did he really win the principle? An experienced missionary in Africa opined that Farther Hillman and others were ready to overturn the whole system to make room for the Masai, who are a dying race. The Masai are a proud tribe of cattle herders (and cattle thieves) with a long history of war and conquest. They are repulsively dirty and insect-ridden, undernourished and ravaged by tuberculosis and syphilis. Probably they are a dying race. Are they entitled to have the gospel proclaimed to them before extinction? The Masai do not really deserve to have the system overturned for their sake; but they make it impossible for us to evade the question whether we really proclaim the gospel to all nations. One wonders how well

Clovis and his Franks would compare with the Masai. Is it their polygamy or their stout refusal to wear pants which makes them unfit for the gospel? Do we believe that they must become European before they can become Christian?

To raise the question does not imply an encouragement of polygamy. We have noticed that the advance of civilization will take care of that. The question is whether we make a cultural change a condition of faith and baptism. I am not sure that we do, but I am concerned enough to ask. The request is simply that moral theologians examine the question anew without prejudice and with some attention to the study of society and culture. I believe that it is not merely a question of polygamy, but of the total identity of the Roman (European) Catholic Church with a determined culture. If this identification has been made, one may remark that the Masai are not the only dying race. Perhaps they are entitled to some of the crumbs that fall from the tables of the masters. I suppose the thing that impressed me most about the Catholic Church in Africa is its general failure to achieve a distinctively African identity. The African episcopacy and clergy are more thoroughly Romanized than the European missionaries, and they show little desire for Africanism. One will hear more drums at Mass in the United States than one will in Tanzania. In recently liberated countries the Catholic Church is still the most thoroughly colonial operation. My parting remark to my last audience in Africa was that I had heard a great deal about *uhuru*. I asked them whether I was to understand that *uhuru* had reference only to politics and culture. The rather positive response led me to hope that the colonial church of Africa will not endure much beyond another generation.

Chapter Nineteen

# WHEN MORE IS EXPECTED, SILENCE IS SERIOUS

SOME FRIENDS and colleagues have recently thrown a book at me with a challenge to comment upon it. The book is *The Silence of Pius XII*, by Carlo Falconi (Boston: Little, Brown. 430 pp. $10.00). Frankly the challenge displeases me, and I respond more from pugnacity than from principle. Probably enough years have passed for me to say without fear of physical harm that I never found Pius XII a sympathetic figure; but sympathy has nothing to do with the judgment of a man who had to meet an unparalleled and unprecedented historical crisis. There was simply no book on how a Pope should meet the Second World War; and works like this one suggest that there is still no book. A man responds to such crises according to his already formed character and habits; and if Pius XII did not come through World War II without blemish, I cannot think of any world figure, secular or religious, who did. He is not credited with such things as the bombings of Dresden, Hamburg and Hiroshima, nor with the policy of unconditional surrender. Pius XII, unlike the secular leaders of his time, is blamed for what he did not do, not for what he did do; and such assessment of blame implies an accurate judgment of what he could do. One who is unsympathetic to Pius XII might say that a man who obviously enjoyed power as much as he did should have used the power he thought he had.

137

Signore Falconi does not make my task any easier by his claim in his preface that his work is not polemical, but an objective and constructive discussion. Having said this, he writes a book in which hostility to Pius XII has been exceeded, to my knowledge, only by Rolf Hochhuth. The interest of the book (and one must be deeply interested to lay out a sawbuck) lies principally in the fact that it does not deal with the Jewish holocaust, but with two other areas less extensively treated in English: occupied Poland under German administration and the Croatian treatment of Serbs. Falconi claims to have access to a large number of documents not available before 1965, the date of the Italian original of this book. Much of this horror story was unknown to me, but I am not a specialist in World War II history. Falconi's thesis for both areas is that Pius XII knew, that he was urged to speak, that he could have spoken, that he ought to have spoken. He believes, as I also believe, that in certain situations it is not relevant whether one expects one's speech to change the situation. The obligation to speak sometimes does not arise from the hope of success but from some more basic obligation. There is some validity to the principle that silence means consent. I believe this principle has an application to one who claims the office of supreme moral teacher which it does not have for me. The moral situation in which Pius XII found himself was at least as urgent as the moral situations which later educed his allocution to the midwives of Rome and his letter to the Superior General of the Jesuits on smoking.

Once this is said, it is recognized as hindsight, the same kind of hindsight which one applies to one's own speech or silence in the past. There is a venerable superstition that speech is a risk, but silence is always safe. A story was told about the late Cardinal Spellman, doubtlessly fictitious, that he had a large fish mounted in his office on the wall behind his chair, with this motto: "If I had kept my mouth shut I would not be here." The late Cardinal did not follow this motto when dealing with the late Mrs. Eleanor Roosevelt. Speaking is a risk; silence is just as much a risk. F. M. Cornford once wrote with surpassing irony that inaction, of course, can have no consequences. What is true is that the consequences of inaction are often not recognized until the nonactor is dead; and that it is very difficult to pin a particular effect on inaction. When we deal with the Holy See we deal with an office which does not admit to mistakes; and it is not the only office in the world which claims infallibility in practice. To criticize its inaction or action is irreverent; it suggests that the Vicar of Christ blew one.

Falconi does not claim that the speech of Pius XII could have saved several million lives, Gentile as well as Jew; no one knows how much power the Pope has in such situations. I think even the late Joseph Stalin would have conceded that he has some. The apologists for Pius XII have generally pleaded that he was powerless in the situations of World War II. The image projected by Pius XII was never the image of a powerless man; I find this apology unconvincing. In all fairness I find Falconi's explanation unconvincing too. Falconi presents several reasons in combination why the Pope chose not to speak to clear moral abominations: his pessimism about the reception of his message, his fear of Communism as the supreme menace, his preoccupation with the survival and the status of the Catholic Church, his Germanophilia and his confidence in diplomacy. This is quite a docket, and the published utterances of Pius XII furnish support for most of them. If one admits that these are proved character traits of Pius XII, one still does not know whether one or all of them influenced him in his handling of the Polish and the Croation problems. What emerges from the docket is that it contains nothing but worldly factors.

If Pius XII dealt with politics on the level of worldly wisdom, he would not have been the first Pope to do so. It would be out of character with the Pope whose portraits were so often said to emit an atmosphere of the spiritual and the otherworldly, but not out of harmony with the tradition of the office. One may wonder what led us to expect anything but worldly wisdom; and when the question is asked, I think one must recognize that the moral status of the Papacy has risen since Pius IX. Add to this the magnitude of the moral crisis of the Second World War, and one sees that we expected something other than tired diplomacy, of which Washington, London and Moscow were furnishing all that was necessary. The Pope as an uncommitted leader of a supranational church could speak with an independent moral leadership which no one else could exhibit. If it did not work, it would be remembered now that he had spoken. He did not speak, and it is remembered now that he did not.

The historian and the theologian, reviewing the topic after twenty years have passed, may judge that the weight of morality and prudence were on the side of speech. This judgment ought to be objective in the sense that it imputes no motives to Pius XII for the decision he made. We do not and cannot know that the weight which we recognize could have been recognized by him; and those who have not been in a similar situation do not know how the crisis of the moment obscures the calm processes of thought. We historians and theologians are not conscious of any immediate practical effects of our decision about the action of Pius XII; about the worst thing we have to fear is a bad review. Without personal criticism such a judgment implies that Pius XII missed greatness at that moment in his life when only greatness was enough to fulfill the mission of the See of Rome. The vision of power dimmed the vision of witness.

The theologian must be concerned with this problem because it is a problem of the exercise of the teaching office of the church. The church claims to teach with a kind of authority which no other church or teaching body claims. With this claim there goes a responsibility which lies on no other church or teaching body. Pius XII asserted his teaching authority as vigorously as any Pope in the nineteenth and twentieth centuries. One way of describing this office is to call it the right and the duty of proclaiming the Gospel to all nations. This phrase is used in Canon 1322, #2. Falconi makes it clear that it was not proclaimed to the governments of Germany and Croatia; that is the area treated in the book, and the statement is not meant to be exhaustive. At what point does it become Christian prudence to refrain from proclaiming the Gospel? The theological literature I have collected in my study does not tell me; one piece of literature, the New Testament, speaks of a point at which the preacher when he is not heard should shake the dust of the unbelieving place from his feet (Matthew 10:14; Mark 6:11; Luke 9:5 + 10:11). Paul is reported to have done this twice (Acts 13:51 + 18:6). Pius XII is not reported to have done this. Formal unbelief is taken rather seriously in the New Testament.

A few years ago I had an exchange of letters with a person of some authority and stature in religion. In the course of the exchange the question of proved American barbarism in Vietnam came up; and I may add that the evidence has now mounted to a point where no one can seriously question it. The person responded that a religious superior whose jurisdiction crosses national boundaries cannot afford to appear to take sides in war. I see what he meant; I dare say Pius XII must have said the same thing more than once in his councils. There is no doubt that a statement would have been seized by the allied powers, whose political principles did not differ notably enough from the principles of Herr Hitler, and used as propaganda. One wonders where one begins to take sides, and at what point an affirmation of basic Christian morality is to take sides. Falconi has remarked that a few stray bombs on Rome elicited a response from Pius XII that terror in Poland and Croatia did not. This, it seems, was not taking sides.

The proclamation of basic Christian morality, even in general terms, will always involve taking sides against those who do not believe in basic Christian morality. Had Pius XII spoken about the terrors of the Nazi policies, he would have had to say something about certain military practices employed by the allied powers. Except for the bombing of Rome he maintained supreme objectivity between the contenders. In fact the church has learned to leave politics to the politicians, who when pressed will deny that morality has anything to do with politics. Most of the time they are right. Is the teaching office of the church competent to speak in those delicate areas where morality touches public policy? If speech were not urgent upon the teaching office during the Second World War, then it is hard to think of any crisis in which speech would be urgent. The theologian must go back to his books and work on a definition of the duty of the church to proclaim the Gospel to all nations; the right of the church to do this seems to have been sufficiently affirmed and discussed. The duty of the proclamation of the Gospel has often included the danger that some one would get killed. Jesus himself said that this danger was nearest to the proclaimers. He said in the same context that the proclaimer must have some trust in the Father, who can do things impossible to diplomacy.

May one withhold the proclamation of the Gospel in order to save innocent lives? And I do not mean one's own life. Not even Hochhuth has suggested that Pius XII was protecting himself. I suspect that Pius XII must have put his own problem in such terms as this; I think it puts the problem in its most acute form. As the question is put it admits no answer; and for that reason one suspects that it is a false position of the question. From the beginning of the church, as we have observed, the proclamation of the Gospel has been risky. The risk is never an excuse for suppressing the Gospel. What assurance can we have that silence will save innocent lives?

The pilgrim church can learn much from its experience in the Second World War. One wonders whether it has learned anything. The vacuum of moral leadership which Pius XII thought he could not afford to fill is still there. The church, in spite of the weakness of its moral stature in the world at large, can still fill the vacuum as no one else can. The response of the world to John XXIII showed that more is still expected of the Papacy than of other agencies.

*Chapter Twenty*

# OBEDIENCE, SUBSTITUTE FOR VIRTUE

**A** CERTAIN embarrassment of riches at the moment of this writing makes the task difficult rather than easy. Theological issues are by no means dead or even moribund; but a number of present issues, in spite of their interest or even urgency, are too large and too complex for discussion here. I choose therefore to enlarge upon an issue raised by James Forest in a review of a book written by Ed Rice about Thomas Merton (*Commonweal*, 1/22/71, 402).

The discussion begins with Rice's revelation that Merton was recently forbidden to write any more about peace. Merton responded in private correspondence with vigor (". . . these people in all the depths of their prejudices and their self-complacency . . .") but decided against breaking the affair open because it would be taken as a witness against the peace movement. This leads Forest (not Rice) to conclude that Merton believed a vow carefully entered into had a weight that precluded disobedience: ". . . an obedience rooted in love could not help but be beneficial in the end." I am sure that the history of the censorship of the writings of Thomas Merton would add some interesting pages to a most unsavory chronicle, and possibly could hasten the end of this practice, which I have elsewhere called basically irrational and immoral; but censorship is not my target here. My question is whether Merton really attached

143

to obedience the nearly sacramental virtues which Forest attaches to it, and whether he was right if he did.

The question is not merely a question of obedience within religious communities. Gabriel Moran has recently pronounced an obituary over religious obedience which a number of indignant correspondents declared premature. Yet the correspondents seemed to assume that religious life would survive by demanding less than the classic model of obedience, often described in the words of Ignatius Loyola as "the staff in the old man's hand" or "like a dead body." Possibly this is an archaic question. The question of how far one must go with the organization is not archaic, nor is it permanently solved in principle. It never will be. Membership in any organization, including the Roman Catholic Church, includes a toleration of evil to a degree which only the individual person can define. Only in such cases as the one in which Merton found himself does anyone ever suggest that cooperation with evil directly contributes to the achievement of good. One wonders why. Cooperation with evil is tolerated because the evil is conceived to be a by-product of some good. One may tolerate it as long as one's contribution to evil is what is called indirect; and any moralist will tell you that not stopping what you cannot stop is indirect.

One may too easily think that he cannot stop or hinder evil, or observe that his responsibility is no greater than the responsibility of anyone else. One may here think of the rich man who was buried in hell for not doing anything. I am reminded almost daily of the national wickedness in Vietnam. Many of my fellow citizens have passed the point of what they consider legitimate tolerance. Yet I can no more share in the enterprise of the bombers than I can share in the Vietnam operation. Whatever these people are promoting, it is not peace; with them I can refuse to cooperate. But the United States takes money from me to spend on a wicked operation. This problem I have not solved, largely because I think I have channels in which to express myself. Ethically the war in Vietnam was no more odious than the Mexican and Spanish wars and the wars

against the American Indians. That these happened is no reason that Vietnam should happen; but it is difficult to look for
a nation whose citizenship would not soil one's hands. The easy
solution is not dynamite but emigration; but would that solve
the problem?

The point is worth dwelling upon because I see so many of
my fellow citizens laying the blame upon the Pentagon or the
State Department or Richard Nixon (after Lyndon Johnson)
and refusing to see the fact that the Vietnam war was an expression of the will of the people of the United States. We are so
schooled to think that the will of the majority is the will of God
that we are unable to cope with a wicked majority. I said emigration is one choice; another is to do what one can to restore
the citizens of the United States to some sense of honor and
decency. No such restoration will occur unless it is the work
of the citizens of the United States. I wish to point out here that
no one attaches a sacramental value to obedience to the will
of the people of the United States expressed through their duly
constituted authorities, unless it be those authorities themselves
or those who are their hirelings. I add the last phrase because
I have just read an almost amusing account of the efforts of one
couple to withhold their telephone tax. The IRS response to
this operation will be written in the American version of *The
Rise and Fall of the Third Reich.* It must be understood that
military men, secret police and civil servants are all of a piece,
whether they work for Adolf Hitler, John Kennedy, or Richard
Nixon. They have no conscience because they need no conscience; the government, which they identify with no hesitation as the will of the people, is their conscience. If the government is wicked—well, love it or leave it, kid. No tyranny can
survive without a sufficient number of finks; I observe that we
have the sufficiency.

Let us return to the sacramental value of obedience and to
the particular case from which this meandering discussion took
off. Let us discuss the problem of Merton and his superiors
as moral theologians, not as preachers, which means that we
talk about the objective act, not motives. I am willing to stip-

ulate that the Abbot of Gethsemane has more authentic holiness in his little finger than I have in my fat head. We have only Merton's letter as reported by Ed Rice, and the quotation is ". . . the orders are no more writing about peace." I am sure the orders were more detailed than that, but let the Abbot give his version if he wants to be understood and forgiven. A moral theologian cannot read this version of the orders without judging that the orders are objectively a mortal sin. I say this because peace is an essential component of the gospel of our Lord and Savior, Jesus Christ. There is no conceivable situation in which one Christian may forbid another to proclaim the essential components of the gospel.

At this point James Forest escapes me. After his beautiful and touching recognition of the sacramental value of obedience paid to bastards, he goes on to remark that it was not the end of Merton's writing about peace anyway. And I may add that the quotations of Merton's observations about both the orders and those who issued them are far from the model of that docile submission which is sometimes called a holocaust; and about these things I have some information. Obedience ceases to be a virtue if you do not keep your mouth shut. What I am pushing is the overturning of this thesis. I propose that obedience is not a virtue but a substitute for virtue, and that keeping one's mouth shut about it is vicious.

In all probability this thesis, like so much of what I have been saying is addressed to a situation which no longer exists. I suspect that the obedience of the dead body and the old man's staff is as dead as the body even in religious communities, and this can only be a gain. If one does not understand how the principle has canonized incompetence, then forget it. I thought James Forest did understand this, and his remark surprised me. It must be understood that the traditional obedience obliged the subjects to something sinful more often than either the subjects or their superiors recognized; and the principle made moral examination of the commands impossible. I remember one religious superior, now deceased many years, who said with a seriousness verging on sanctimoniousness, "Obedience is sacred." I was too young and naive to ask whether anything else was sacred—love and compassion, for instance. I now know that nothing else was sacred. I do not think that even this misguided man, who did not create the manner of life which he accepted, deserved to live without love and to die without compassion, as he did. Can it be Christian morality to support a way of life in which love and compassion become dispensable virtues? Will someone show me the sacramental value of treating people as things?

One cannot leave the topic without adverting to the encyclical *Humanae Vitae*. More than anything else this has compelled many priests and laity to ask themselves whether obedience has a sacramental value. Many have decided that it has not, and the decision has taken many of them further than they were prepared to go. It is indeed a defect of the traditional obedience that it compelled them to go so far. Some have looked at the problems of living persons, problems which can only be compounded beyond solution if they are morally obliged to a choice between continence and more children than they can support. Some have looked at this human problem and decided that if this suffering is the price of maintaining the image of the magisterium, they cannot support the magisterium. They appear to be motivated by love and compassion; to these, and not to obedience, a quasi-sacramental value may be attached. We need them more than we need obedience, more than we need the image of the infallible teacher.

## Chapter Twenty-One

# CATHOLIC HIGHER EDUCATION: HONESTY OVER AUTHORITY

**T**HESE COMMENTS are being written from a hospital bed. This is not intended to be an apology for any lapses in style which probably will occur due to the fact that it is not really being written but dictated through an electronic instrument. Nor is it intended to be an occasion to give the public a recital of the ills and pains which God's kindly providence has seen fit to visit on me briefly in respect to my sins. In fact it is no more than a temporary repair and maintenance job, we hope, and I should be back in circulation before long. I am sorry to say that I can render no comfort to those who hope that there is nothing trivial about it.

I hesitate to present some reflections on the problems of Catholic education. Catholic education has been submitted now to the diagnosis of every major and minor pundit in the country. The experts are gathered around its feeble form like the surgeons around the patient, or perhaps like the surgeons around the corpse preparing for the autopsy. I have no prescription for the ills of Catholic education and I no longer have what I had up to a few years ago—a fairly sunny optimism that Catholic education would survive this crisis as it has survived so many. So my reflections on Catholic education mainly have to do with why this optimism has given way to a fairly realistic but a fairly grim estimate of its future. In particular, I am interested in higher education, that part of Catholic education which provides me with a livelihood. In saying that it provides me with a livelihood I do not wish to take a purely personal and gainful appraisal of Catholic education. It has also furnished me for all my adult life with something which I believed was worth working for. I would not wish to lose this dedication.

My reflections have been stimulated by a couple of articles I have read over the last several months at random. One of which in particular gave me a new and rather distressing insight into the present and the future of Catholic colleges. At the moment I am able to cite neither author nor journal, but they are the occasions of my reflections rather than the source of them. I was impressed by the article of a Catholic college graduate, I believe of no more than ten years ago, which manifested a deep and quite vindictive hatred toward the religious community of men which operates this institution. No good will be served by naming the institution nor the community although I suspect both will emerge for the discerning, especially for the discerning who happen to remember the same article.

The institution in question is of the university level, it is old and well established, it has thousands of alumni in business and the professions in some of our largest cities. I say the article exhibited a degree of hatred which surprised me. I am not unfamiliar with the institution or with the religious order in question. Such hatred has never been entirely unknown in my experience; in fact there are some members of the community which operated the high school which I attended—the Jesuits —whom I still hate after over forty years and quite some time after they are dead. I hate them simply because they were hateful. But these few were the exceptions in my experience. Most of the Jesuit fathers who were engaged in the educational enterprise in those days were honest and kindly even though at times they may have been narrow and unenlightened and intolerant. These qualities are rarely combined with genuine honesty and kindness and it is safe to describe these men as really having very little of these disagreeable traits. A few of them had quite an ample supply of these disagreeable traits but they were so few that they did not leave a lasting impression of themselves as typical of the Jesuits. The writer apparently found no other kind in his experience which is much more recent than mine.

I am not taking the writer as a completely reliable witness of the priests whom he met. I would say that the author manifested prejudice as much as any priest whom he might have met manifested narrowness and intolerance. The largest single item in his charge was a long encounter with a university president who, to put it most politely, threw his weight around somewhat—less politely, he was a bully. I knew the university president in question. He is now dead and I found the story not incredible. At the same time I do not believe this story, even if it may have happened, to be truly representative of the man. We have, however, all had the experience of the single incident which turns someone completely off. This was such an experience. The writer closed his mind to the president, to the university and to the entire religious community associated with the university.

This suggests another phenomenon which I have been compelled to notice over the last ten to fifteen years. The writer observes that this university will never receive a cent of contribution from him. I have heard a large number of Catholic college graduates, both men and women, say this. I have heard them say, in addition, that their sons and daughters, when the time comes, will not attend the old school or, indeed, any Catholic school. What I believe is statistically verified, although I have no statistics at hand at present, is that alumni giving among Catholic institutions is notoriously much less than the great private institutions of the American educational tradition. To my knowledge, with the exception of the University of Notre Dame, most Catholic universities and colleges look elsewhere than their alumni for the money which they need to meet their regular charges, let alone to think of any expansion. The number of alumni who speak with this kind of hostility is large enough to depress me if I were engaged in fund raising. It ought to be enough to depress those who are in the managerial councils of our Catholic higher institutions and, for all I know, it is a matter of concern.

But the concern does not seem to reach the regular level of teaching and student relations. Not all of these alumni speak with the bitterness of the one I mentioned. After all, most of them are not professional writers nor do they all have a horror story like the writer, although many can give you similar horror stories on demand. The reasons for the dislike which they express are quite varied and this is again rather distressing than encouraging. One has to conclude, I fear, that Catholic institutions as a group have not succeeded in winning the lasting affection of the men and women whom they have educated for adult life. Why they have failed cannot be analyzed at the moment by me. Perhaps it can be analyzed by no one. If this vague impression, however, rests on a solid body of fact which can be observed, then Catholic education has failed to win the people whom it needs most and who of all else it ought to have as its friends rather than as indifferent or as its enemies.

There may be one single factor which contributes to this hatred which deserves study. When I suggest this I do not mean that we have necessarily solved the problem. It also may be that the suggestion I make is not very close to the center of the problem, but as I said, this kind of hatred is not entirely unknown in earlier generations. It showed itself less, but it did show itself. I propose that as important as anything else in winning the lasting dislike or even hatred of a student is the assumption by the university (whether by its administration or its faculty or both) of an authority which is thought to be the authority of the church rather than of the teacher: the claim of the Catholic university to be an extension of the teaching authority of the church. This permits the university or its teachers to impose the truth on its students with the same authority with which the church imposes the faith upon its members. I would not say that this is a conscious confusion of roles but I certainly observed it in my teachers years ago and I observe it in some of my colleagues at present. And I do not wish to say that I observe it only in my older colleagues at present. It permits the teacher to exhibit all the vices which in the academic world are associated with authoritative teaching.

The academic world, on principle, rejects authoritative teaching, although it has its authoritative teachers as well as the Catholic system does. But in the Catholic system the authoritative teacher is not rejected. He is rather regarded as a true copy of the divine heavenly teacher and the man who best fulfills the ideal of the Catholic teacher. The vices which this ideal not only permits, but fosters, are the suppression of discussion and of criticism, the dishonest concealment of certain areas of study, termination of questions when they become too difficult to answer, the rewarding of the docile and the uncritical combined with the punishment of the intelligent, the critical and the alert. I was, may God forgive me, a gifted student. I was also an interested and a diligent student and, up to my lights, docile. I had great curiosity and a desire to learn more. One does not forget, even after forty years, the metaphorical slap in the face which is given to the inquiring student who in all good faith proposes a question which he learns only later the teacher not only cannot answer but will not permit to be asked. I might have come to the same conclusion that the writer mentioned above did; I always felt that such men were really not representative of a Catholic teacher or of the Catholic Church and that the question which they angrily rejected as blasphemous or heretical might be met by some other person who would deal with it in the spirit in which it was asked. In fact, one almost never found such men. The answers had to be sought out in one's own reading and one's own thinking or discussion with one's fellows.

One may think that my explanation of why I did not rebel more deeply against such things is not very sound. I must remind the objector that in my generation we had not learned to question the teaching authority of the church as such. Such tactics would leave one with the vague dissatisfaction that the teaching authority should not need to stoop to such means to defend itself but we really did not know enough about the teaching authority of the church and its use to reach an idea of how it should behave. Many of my contemporaries who went to secular big name colleges came out of the process with a permanent loss of faith. This was always a cause of great indignation to the faculty members of Catholic universities who loved to point to such institutions as hotbeds of atheism and immorality. As a matter of fact, the shock of a Catholic student at being treated like a human being instead of something that came out from under the rug was so great that many never recovered from it. The rest of us believed that there was a church and a teaching authority worth preserving and that while we may have met some of its less noble representatives, there was no more reason for leaving the church because of such people than there was for leaving the United States because of certain political figures who inhabited the country.

More offensive to most students of Catholic schools in those days was the assumption of authority over one's private life and personal decisions. Again, we were hardly tigers in our opposition to this. The Catholic school did not pretend to be anything else than it was. It advertised to parents that it would protect their young, masculine and feminine, from the dangers and temptations of the world by restricting their contacts with the world and by giving them as little freedom of decision in meeting the world as they could possibly hold them down to. For most students ideas were not important. Freedom of entertainment was much more important. They did not accept this, but it was a game which they knew that ultimately they would win. The police power of most Catholic institutions was not up to the ingenuity of the students. And the students regarded it as a sort of training period which was of brief duration and would end in adult freedom. This was the way in which one reached adult freedom. Yet this left behind itself some very deep hatreds as well.

The writer cited in his encounter with the university president was dealing with a matter of discipline not with a matter of ideas. As he described it, the university president dealt with him as a child and even though in those terms, dealt with him unfairly. I said that I found this credible. I doubt that this is the last experience that the writer has had with those who deal with him unfairly. If it is, I would really like to know where he lives and works. It might be worthwhile exploring the possibility of moving there. I do not pretend to justify actions such as those which he described by saying that they prepare one for similar actions to be experienced later, although if one wants to talk about education as including an exposure to the harsh realities of life, unfairness is certainly one of its harsh and frequent realities. The writer may have asked more of the university than at the moment he asked of the world in which he lived. To ask more could be unfair as well. At the same time, I once turned my back on an educational officer and left the room unbidden at what I considered unfairness. I could have been expelled. At the moment I did not care.

I have observed that Catholic alumni do not respond with gifts in the way in which great private institutions expect their alumni to respond and in which their alumni do respond. It is no longer possible to comfort ourselves with the feeling that we are educating the sons of the poor and that they do not earn enough surplus to contribute to their university. Many of them do earn enough but they are not contributing. My question is not so much as to whether this can or ought to be changed, my question is whether an educational institution, traditionally known as alma mater, which leaves such a permanently sour relation between itself and its nurslings ought to be supported either by them or by anyone else. It would seem possible that the major interest in institutions is not the students. What the major interests may be I do not know. Some of my colleagues would grumble survival and let it go at that. But the institutions can only survive by their friends. Without friends they have no hope of survival and, I suggest, possibly no reason for survival. It may not be, to repeat once more, merely a question that the faculties and the administration of the universities and colleges are more interested in controlling the students than in loving them. But I think this is a fair description of many people and many institutions.

Let me add that I dislike saying this at a point in history when the undergraduates of so many colleges and universities seem to be doing as much as they can to render themselves un-lovable. At such a time I suppose we shall show our adulthood by rising above the level at which our students present them-selves. Surely such a self-interested group has rarely appeared in such numbers in college enrollment since the University of Paris first opened its door, whenever that was. And in this af-firmation of the priority of the student as the object of interest, I have no intention of affirming therewith an identification with the student in all his quality of spoiled brat nor any concession that bad as the institution may be, it will be improved by free love, free drugs and free credits. It would hardly be an im-provement to trade in one form of lack of integrity for another which, in fact, some of our Catholic institutions seem bent on doing.

But whether one treats a student as a student and not as an object, as a learner and not as an object of indoctrination, as a person and not merely as a source of income does not depend on the character of the student. It depends on the character of the university. If the student is unworthy of the treatment, that is the misfortune of both the student and the university. But the university at least will not have to criticize itself for giving the student less than he as a human being deserves.

I conclude by reflecting that the Catholic higher educational enterprise with all its faults, has really meant too much, not only to the church, but also to the community of the United States to be allowed to die without some major effort to pre-serve it. It will be done in, as it has been remarked, by its friends if it is done in at all. But these will be the friends who will insist that the Catholic higher educational system be used for their purposes. It does not make much difference what these purposes are.

Strictly speaking, to think of the Catholic college as the arm of the teaching church at one time was a noble ideal. We know

now it is dead wrong and that unchecked it will kill the university just as surely as politics has killed the universities in Latin America. We know that the integrity of the system depends not so much on the faith or the orthodoxy of those in the system —these are qualities which run through all activities of human life, not just education. The integrity depends on qualities specific to the educational process.

After most of an adult life spent in this endeavor, I have about decided that we will have to settle without any complicated formulae on intellectual honesty as the thing which the university ought to exhibit. We will also have to accept, I fear, that those who represent this quality have to be those who teach in these institutions. If they do not exhibit it, it is hardly to be expected that anyone else will and if they do not exhibit it, then there is no salvation for Catholic education. Enough people have been doing what they could to extirpate intellectual honesty in Catholic higher education for a long enough time to make one believe that just possibly they cannot succeed. In a desperate cause, desperate means have to be attempted. And they will be attempted if anyone believes that the objective is worth working for.

*Chapter Twenty-Two*

# THEOLOGY OF DEFECTION

IT OCCURS to me that there ought to be some theology of defection; it would be the reverse of the theology of vocation. If the number of those who leave and the number of those who do not enter is as large as it appears, the church may be facing a serious decline in the number of her professional workers just at the time when new needs and new works are clearly emerging. At the moment the church is not equipped to replace these professionals with others. Unless she finds replacements or halts the outflow, she will meet the challenges of the world and of the Second Vatican Council with insufficient personnel.

We shall use the traditional word "defection," in spite of the fact that the word begs the question. Apart from the failure of health, neither the dioceses nor the religious orders have ever admitted that there is a good reason for anyone to leave the seminary, the religious profession, or holy orders. Any departure is a defection, a failure, on the part of the one who leaves. The organization remains serenely perfect with no responsibility for the defection. We have always known that this posture is indefensible, but because of our commitment to the organization we have not tried to find the correct posture. If defections could be analyzed by psychological and sociological methods—a dissertation topic for some ambitious young Ph.D. candidate—I suspect we should find that few if any cases are unmixed, and that the organization is rarely innocent when de-

159

fection occurs. Whether the dioceses and the orders have the moral courage to support such a study I do not know.

The fact is that an unusual number of priests and religious and an unusual number of potential candidates are voting with their feet, the only thing they have to vote with, and they are not telling us why. There has been no articulate spokesman for defection except that of English theologian, Charles Davis. It has been proved dangerous to agree with Charles Davis, and since I am much more chicken than tiger, I shall not agree with him. I shall merely point out that in all the brouhaha about Davis no one took the trouble to deny the truth of what he said. Unless one takes Davis seriously one is not facing the problem of defection; and this has nothing to do with the truth of what he said. It has everything to do with what he said as a witness of his own mind and heart; for he surely spoke for many who leave. He even spoke for many who have not left. These sentiments are widespread, so widespread that simple denial is now meaningless. If these people are wrong the truth must be shown by some rational means. If they are right, a condition exists which they cannot correct; they can only run. If, as is ultimately most probable, the truth lies somewhere between extremes, then nothing but Christian love and honesty will disclose the truth and cure what ails us. Further name-calling can do nothing but widen the breach which any but a congenital idiot must see opening. And it will open wider if the organization wipes its lips, wraps its mantle of self-righteousness about it, and says, "I have done no wrong."

More than a few people think that the Davis affair suggests that the organization has done something wrong, and that the organization knows it. It is not unfounded to think that on certain high prelatial levels insecurity has been manifested. There is a fear that power is being lost, the traditional power for which no substitute has been found. If these prelates talked to more people, they might feel even more insecure. With respect to the problem under discussion, insecurity attracts no one to a permanent religious attachment to an organization; this ought to be so self-evident as to need no discussion. There are still enough young men and women ready to dedicate themselves to the total service of Christ in his church, but not to total subjection of wavering leadership.

The facts, poorly known as they are, suggest that the priestly and religious vocation no longer has the attraction it had a few years ago. There are several candidates for the role of the villain in this piece, but most of them do not qualify. The growth of worldliness and the love of ease simply have nothing to do with it. The nation has never been so prosperous as it was after the Second World War, and no notable drop in vocations was manifested during this period. The young people who join the Peace Corps and similar operations are not suffering from worldliness and the love of ease, and those who try to join these operations for a thrill are screened out. This feeble excuse supposes that there have been times when the world was not worldly.

Celibacy is bound to come up for discussion, although I hold a certain dislike of the topic. Traditionally, defectors have always been shrugged off as incontinent, and we continent could afford to patronize them. My own feeling is that this is a decision which men and women should be left to make for themselves and that it should not be part of a package deal. I suspect that this is the direction in which history will move, but I am not trying to nudge it very hard. What can be forgotten, and what Charles Davis brought up, is that without a very substantial integration in the priestly or religious life a terrible loneliness can set in. I do not say a perfect integration, because that is impossible. But there is an indefinable point at which one feels entirely alone. Do the defectors leave because they fall in love, or do they fall in love because they are leaving? It is not simple. Celibacy can be proposed as a barren life, it can be demonstrated by example as a barren life, and it can turn barren. What I have seen of "spiritual" literature and counseling indicates that there is rarely a positive approach to celibacy. It is a virtue which is perfected by not doing something. Very few have ever accepted celibacy as anything except part of the package. If they are less ready to accept it now, it could be because their observation of celibates has led them to think they do not want to be like that. It could be something else, but it deserves some thought. And it may as well be added that celibacy is the renunciation of marriage, not of sex. I betray no secrets when I observe that there has always been room in the church—more in some other countries than in this—for celibates who could not live alone, as long as they did not marry and kept it quiet. If this is the way we prefer it, no one should be surprised that decent people generally abhor it. But I doubt that this is a major factor in the vocation-defection crisis, although this estimate may have to be revised.

It can be suggested that it is the disintegration and the loneliness which is the problem rather than the search for love which results from the loneliness. Love is a larger reality than marriage, and one who finds love in his vocation is unlikely, as far as one can be sure of human choice, to seek love in marriage. This is not to omit the possibility that one can continue to survive without love; he is not a very beautiful sight, and he inspires no one to do what he did, but he can survive. I am aware that this sounds rather trite, but there are some basic realities about which it is hard to be anything but trite. Does the life of professional service of the church exhibit love, either to those within it or to those who contemplate it as a vocational choice? It certainly does, but it can be hidden; one who could find it in some situations—since no one sees the whole church at once—would be a very certain candidate. Perhaps we have attracted more vocations than we should; perhaps we have expected from many what only a few can give. Perhaps we shall have to commit much of our work to the laity; the turn in the figures may be a turn toward reality. There are certain areas of the church in which I could with good conscience advise no one to seek a vocation.

But has the church as a profession suddenly ceased to exhibit the reality of the community of love which it exhibited, shall we say, up to 1965—that is to say, up to the Second Vatican Council? Shall we blame the Council for the vocation crisis? To some extent we can, at least indirectly. The Council did open some vague but new and promising prospects for the future. These were inspiring, even exciting. The time lag in realizing these prospects is obvious; and it is hardly a great discovery to observe that youth is impatient. I do not know why they should be more impatient; they will surely live to see many of the Council's projects realized, and I surely will not. But they must make a vocational decision now; they may have confidence that the official leadership will move, but they have no time to wait for it to move. Rome moves slowly—that is the ecclesiastical adage. If it does not move more rapidly, it may find when it does move that there is no one left to move with it. I will hazard the guess that an evident and quick, even hasty and ill-considered jump toward the things proposed by the Second Vatican Council would cure the vocation crisis sooner than any other single action.

A colleague remarked that in my own writing and speaking about the glories of the lay vocation I was actually denigrating the priestly and religious vocation so that no one would be attracted to it. I do not think my fellows and I can be invoked as contributing to the crisis. But once the lay vocation is conceived as the service of the church, the priestly and religious vocation ceases to be the only way in which one can serve the church. I submit that it is both the attraction of the lay apostolate and the unfavorable image of the priestly and religious apostolate which, taken together, may have something to do with the vocation crisis. The gentlemen who edit such journals as *The Critic* and *Commonweal* conceive that they are engaged in the service of the church as much as the priests who edit *America*. My lay colleagues from De Paul and other Catholic colleges and universities conceive that they serve the church as much as I, as a member of the faculty, do. If they look more closely, they will notice that their service is done without certain inhibitions which they can see in me—not to mention others which they do not see. It will have to be clear to them that these inhibitions are necessary and that they serve a good purpose. I am not sure that it is clear, nor that anyone could make it clear. If one talks about them, things are bound to come out;

if one refuses to talk about them, the listeners fear that the hidden reality is too bad to be discussed.

Traditionally the flow of vocations has been sustained by the acquaintance of young men and women with priests and religious who were contented and who seemed to have found personal fulfillment in their life. I do not believe this type has suddenly disappeared in the last two years. What we have is a generation gap and a movement in the church to something new. I will guess that young people are no longer inspired by a religious career which seems to consist so often in minding the store. Several religious communities have found that their younger members have no interest in just those works which are the traditional works of the community. Interest in the parochial ministry is stimulated by existing and projected new experimental parishes. Young people now have vocational opportunities which were not available when we were their age. They are not attracted by what attracted us. When the new vocational opportunities appear in the church also, but only in the lay apostolate, we have our problem. I believe this touches defections as well as the lack of vocations. The work of a priest or a religious has to be rewarding, but it is not dependent solely on the individual priest or religious that it should be so.

The new movement in the church is a movement toward greater personal freedom. Reviewing the past, one sees that it had to come, and that it should have come sooner; we are fortunate that its coming was not longer delayed. This too is part of the cultural phenomenon, and we cannot annihilate it by saying that it ought not to happen. My experience is that the laity expect priests and religious to renounce some or all of their freedom, and that they even resent it when someone moves toward more freedom. They accept this, if they are unsophisticated, as one of the basic things which they do not understand. The sophisticated take quite another view. But sophisticated or not, they believe that this life of unfreedom is not for them. If they can serve the church with freedom, they would rather serve her with it than without it. This attitude, I suppose, is going to rub off on their children, the potential candidates for the priesthood and the religious life.

Are we pushing the panic button too soon? Is this a passing phase of uncertainty rather than a crisis? Perhaps; many will say so. But phase or crisis, it brings up a number of things which ought to be done in any hypothesis. Restructuring the priesthood and the religious life is overdue. It would be no mistake to do it even if the crisis should turn out to be exaggerated. After all, how could superiors be happy without subjects?

*Chapter Twenty-Three*

# ONE MAN'S REVOLT

JAMES KAVANAUGH, took a look at his outdated church and decided to abandon it. I am not going to write a review of his book, but rather a review of his reviewers; and I feel I have a franchise to do this because I am among the pundits who were quoted in the book's advertising. I thank all those who have written me about this, both those who signed their names (who have received letters of reply) and those who did not (naturally they did not receive letters). When one is approached by a publisher with such a request one knows that anything one writes may be used in advertising. I said (cautiously, I thought) that the best I could hope from the book was that it might bring others to a concern as deep as Kavanaugh's about the question he raises. I should add that one need not express his deep feeling in the language of Kavanaugh; frankly, I thought the book was a sustained scream, which always sets one's nerves on edge in any situation. I would not write in such a tone myself, but that does not prove that no one should. And in the back of my mind was the apprehension that the preachers of sweet reasonableness, of whom I am one, have dispensed so much gooey reasonableness that we may be drowning in soothing syrup. Perhaps nothing can be done unless someone stands up and shouts, "The hell with it." In other words, we sweetly reasonable ones may be the Kerenskys and the Mirabeaus of the impending ecclesiastical revolution. I do not like this thought, but perhaps it is time to share it. Anyway, Kavanaugh has certainly stood up and shouted as described.

I said I wanted to review the reviewers. With a few rare exceptions like Robert Hoyt, practically none of them came to grips with the issues. They came to grips with Kavanaugh. When all is said about the shrill tone of his book, the hard sell campaign of his publishers ("Can you imagine that—that—phony priest on Johnny Carson's show!"), the one-sidedness and the unkindness of his presentation, there is left an ample residue of gut issues which the reviewers chose to ignore. Kavanaugh often achieved in his book a harshness which equals anything he found in the ecclesiastical ogres who have haunted his life; and I must say the reviewers were right in there with more of the same. One suspects that a man who elicits such emotional responses must have rubbed some very sore spots, but one knew this anyway. The high point or the low, depending on your perspective, is in the now frequently repeated allegation that K. is sick. Now I am not personally acquainted with K., and I would regard it as out of my competence to judge whether he is sick. It would surprise me that Simon & Schuster, a group of fairly astute businessmen, would invest so much in the work of a sick man, apart from the ethics of exploiting the sick. K. is angry, which may approach sickness but is not the same thing. But a book review is scarcely the place to discuss the mental health of an author, even if one does know the author personally. A low blow, friends and colleagues, unworthy of you even if you thought it was not unworthy of the object. If K. lowered the tone, you kept it down.

If the man is wrong, for God's sake say so; and this is just what the reviewers did not do, choosing to discuss K.'s warped personality instead. One more warped personality is not a disaster for the church; I know priests and bishops and cardinals who have warped personalities, and we have lived with it a long time. But if there is anything substantial in K.'s charges, cataclysm may be just around the corner. I am ready to admit that the space of a review is too limited for even inadequate discussion, but the reviewers might at least have made a few lunges at the problems. It is just fatuous to say that he said nothing which we have not all known for a long time; by implication we have known it and done nothing, and we intend to continue to do nothing, presumably on the assumption that nothing needs to be done or can be done. It is fatuous to say that action is being taken to correct abuses, admitting cautiously that there may be one or two nonurgent abuses which need correction. It would be so fatuous to say that there is nothing at all to what he wrote that I have heard of no reviewer who said it.

The reviewers missed the strength of Kavanaugh's book, which is that it hit ecclesiastical operations just where they touch persons. It is here that ecclesiastical operations are at their worst; they turn persons into cases. If something is going to be right in the future, why is it not right at the present moment? People who live now are as fully persons and as fully entitled to simple justice, let alone charity, as those of the next generation. People are sacrificed to a system which is under repair; and this inverts the order of finality. The system is for people. The work of the church is not exactly like the paving of a street or the building of a subway or an expressway. We can and do expect people to make detours, to experience long traffic delays, to risk their limbs and their axles in chuckholes. But it does not take a generation to repave an expressway or lay subway tracks; and the lack of these conveniences at the moment does not involve basic decisions concerning human existence. We have been presenting certain things to the faithful as simply matters of heaven or hell, in our belief fairly basic to human existence. Now we tell them changes are coming, but they will please hold the line until we get ready to announce them. And this apart from the fact that many in the church are simply hanging on in the hope that if the changes are postponed long enough the desire for change will disappear; we will outwait them. Kavanaugh does not believe that human wear and tear should be simply accepted as an operational loss, inevitable like the deaths and injuries inherent in the use of the automobile. Somewhere in his twisted mind he has got the idea that every human person is sacred, and that all human persons are equally sacred. Somewhere in my own twisted mind is the same conviction. I read it in a book; I think the New Testament. A difference between us is that he seems close to excluding ecclesiastical prelates from this realm of the sacred. I understand his problem, but I cannot join him in the exclusion. It is a Christian principle that we should love most those who need it most.

So, brother reviewers, by not taking the trouble to deny or discuss the truth of Kavanaugh's charges, you left your readers with the conclusion that he is right but a very bad man. You could not discuss the problems in a more elevated tone. Some of you came close to dismissing concern for persons as sickly sentimentality, and I hope nothing worse happens to you than that someone will dismiss concern for you as sickly sentimentality. You were angry that he said that Catholic theology died somewhere between Thomas and Tarzan, and you want to know why he ignores Rahner, Murray, de Lubac, Congar and the rest of the glorious company. Did you forget that the late John Courtney Murray was forbidden to finish his series on church and state and was forced to get what he could in the only organ which would take it, the acts of the Second Vatican Council? Did you not read in Xavier Rynne that Rahner had to submit all his writings to censorship in Rome? Did you fail to notice that de Lubac and Congar were silent for some years after the "new theology" dustup in 1950? You leave this reader wondering whether you really care very much for Catholic theology. Believe me, if it is great, it is so in spite of obstacles which you either did not know, or think are trivial. Since Murray died I have asked myself whether the church of this generation deserved him.

Now that I have faulted the reviewers for not discussing the issues, someone may wonder whether I am going to discuss them myself. Not in this chapter, nor in any other single chapter. I think I have touched on some elsewhere, and I do not see how I can avoid some others. But I do not intend to ignore them; they are just too many and too big for a quick look. There is room for a few lunges, as suggested above, and these I intend to make. At the moment I can say only this in the space available: From my limited pastoral experience there was not one incident mentioned by Kavanaugh which I found incredible. I suppose this is what my colleagues mean when they say he tells us nothing new. The difference is in the value judgment we make about the importance of such things. I would prefer that we do not call the presentation one-sided and think we have done the job. I suppose one could say that a diagnosis of a cancer of the liver is one-sided; sure his liver is gone, but look at how sound his stomach and his lungs are—he did not smoke cigarettes.

Obviously not everyone will accept the figure of cancer for the situation; and I am not sure that it is the apt figure. Cancer is normally fatal. The church cannot die but she can go through an experience that would kill something else. I think we have a duty to see that she does not have such an experience. An excess of caution here will easily be forgiven. But I would not present renewal as something to be done to forestall an ecclesiastical revolution; the only good reason for renewal is that it is the right thing to do. I have expressed some dire forebodings which may be the effect of advancing years; older people often seem sure that total collapse is near, to be expected shortly after they can reasonably be expected to die. But one is alarmed when the Vatican Secretary of State is quoted as saying that the work of renewal was "happily completed" by the Second Vatican Council. If I am playing Mirabeau, he is trying hard for the role of Marie Antoinette.

If anything could be likened to cancer in the Mystical Body, it would be loss of respect for the individual person, a cooling of Christian love. One weakness of Kavanaugh's book was its anecdotal character; no matter how many anecdotes you heap up, you cannot thence arrive at a valid generalization. Hence the anecdotes are dismissed as not typical; but, as noticed above, the fury which the anecdotes elicit leaves one wondering whether someone has not been hurt by the charges. I have many fewer anecdotes than Kavanaugh, and I cannot arrive at a valid generalization. What I do know is that one such instance is too many. The church will fail in love, because she is not yet the full eschatological reality; but she ought not, and should note every failure and try to find the causes. And this is the only valid generalization I can make; no one will deny its generality. But to be more particular: Is the failure in love due to that thing which others besides Kavanaugh call "the system"? An important part of renewal is a very close look at the system, but not the kind of look which will promise results in twenty years. We priests are responsible to those to whom we minister now, not to those whom some other priests will serve in 1990. I submit that we will make it easier for them to cherish love in 1990 if we see that there is some left to cherish after this year.

Ecclesiastical administration is under suspicion, in fact it is under fire; it has got to clear itself, or its image is gone for good. No one involved in it at any level can take a routine decision now without examining it, unless he wants to become another anecdote for another Kavanaugh. Particular enough? I will be even more particular; the man who finds that the system compels him to be more concerned with sin than with persons, to set rules above people, should in all honesty refuse. He is skating on very thin ice. We can no longer afford the unexamined decision. No one man can remove disrespect for the person, but he can remove himself from sharing in it.

As for you, Father Kavanaugh, wherever you are, I have a few words. I am angry with you for making it so difficult to talk about the things which concern us all very deeply. You let yourself be carried away by your feelings, you spoke harshly in a situation which needed no harshness added. Did you not think that anyone who tries to treat the issues will hear, "You sound just like Kavanaugh"? You have said your piece and renounced any further effort to live with what you find intolerable. This is your personal decision which it is not my business to analyze. But could you not have done it in such a way as to make it possible for us whose personal decision is different to work toward a goal which you apparently think is impossible? You did not show respect for our own freedom of decision; by implication— although I am sure not by intention—you made us all look like lackeys and hirelings, ready to do the king's dirty work as long as we take the king's shilling. You effectively accused us either of stoning or of holding the garments of those who throw the stones. I do not think you really believe this; I think you wrote hastily and carelessly, and as a professional writer I am unhappy with this kind of work. I am disappointed because you did not accomplish what you could have accomplished and what I think you really wanted to accomplish. We need you, and you let us down. You see I am still hopelessly committed to sweet reasonableness; I hang on to my foolish faith in the power of free rational discussion, although it gets harder to hold day by day. I still do not think, and never will, that the way to solve the problems of the church is to get up and shout, "The hell with it."

## Chapter Twenty-Four

# OH, THE MAJESTY
# AND MYSTERY!

**I**T WAS 1959, I think, before anything I had said or written came to the attention of any churchman across the Atlantic who ranks higher than simple priest. I drew attention by a paper on liturgical language read to the Liturgical Congress in Cincinnati. The paper contained no recommendation of a change to the vernacular; with a great caution (which I have but rarely got credit for) I confined myself to a few historical observations that a "liturgical" language is a rare phenomenon in religions, and did not appear in Catholicism until it was fairly well advanced in history. It is hard to believe that this innocent thesis would get out the bloodhounds only eight years ago. The paper is absolutely useless now.

At that time there existed an organization called the Society for the Promotion of the Vernacular in the Liturgy (I think), inspired and largely propelled by the incomparable Irwin St. John Tucker, known to his friends (who surpass number) as Friar Tuck. As far as I know, this is the only society which ever declared itself out of existence because it had achieved its purpose. I do not really think it has to reconstitute itself as the Society for the Maintenance of the Vernacular in the Liturgy, in spite of some manifest dissatisfaction. History is with them, but as long as the history is still in process, a few remarks on this theological problem may be in order.

When I speak of dissatisfaction, I am not thinking of Gommar De Pauw and his followers. It is hard to take Gommar seriously, and the kindest thing I can think of to say about his dedicated followers is that they have abominably bad manners. What really elicits these words is a piece by William Buckley, whom I do take seriously. Should Mr. Buckley see this, he may think I am making fun of him; and I want to assure Mr. Buckley that I know it is dangerous to make fun of him. Unlike Gommar, Buckley is witty, articulate and endowed with an admirable sense of humor. When he makes a point, he makes it sharp. When Mr. Buckley puts into Buckley prose the inarticulate grumblings which one hears in almost any parish, it is time to look out. It is not fair—at least not for me—to say that Buckley represents the past and will be buried with it. Mr. Buckley is younger than I am, and if he is not better preserved he should see his physician as soon as possible. He will be around for quite a while to throw barbs at the new liturgy, unless he loses interest in this target.

To sum up Mr. Buckley's objections is difficult (any professional writer must respect Mr. Buckley's economy of words). But I shall try. The reformed liturgy, he says, is vulgarization. There was majesty and mystery in the Latin which is now gone. The laity do not understand the English any better than they understood the Latin. And—I think most important—congregational worship distracts Mr. Buckley from his own spiritual pursuits. None of these points are without weight.

As to the vulgarization: I do not know whether Mr. Buckley owns a TV set. He ought to, considering the mileage he gets out of this medium. I do not own one nor do I freeload on another set; I simply do not watch TV, and the people who make audience surveys should reach me. If they do, I will tell them frankly that I do not watch TV because I cannot stand the commercials; they revolt me so much that I cannot tell whether the rest of the material is as bad as I hear it is. Anyway, if Mr. Buckley turns on his TV set for as much as thirty minutes a week, he ought to be able to suffer through a Mass in the vernacular. He would say, no doubt, that vulgarization is inevitable on TV but out of place in public worship: it is what the people want. But, Mr. Buckley, it is no more inevitable on TV than it is in worship. The same people who watch TV appear at Mass. That art or spectacle is religious is no insurance against bad taste.

Mr. Buckley appeals to the Cathedral of Chartres. Was he so struck by its Gothic majesty and its unearthly windows that he failed to see the appalling marble pile which some baroque prelate stuck there for a high altar? The incongruity he deplores has been there for a few hundred years. Many of us think that the great cathedrals are museums rather than places for a worshiping community to assemble, but I am not sure of this; one of the most genuinely religious acts I have ever witnessed was a pontifical Mass at Notre Dame in Paris—in Latin, too, Mr. Buckley. But the Gothic of Chartres with its baroque abortion in the middle is a very proper symbol of men at work at worship. The baroque prelate may have been just as devout as the men who built the cathedral—from all I know about the twelfth century, he had an excellent prospect of being more devout. There are just too many people engaged in worship to make it possible to find external forms to suit everybody, and someone must suffer. In his parish, I guess it is Mr. Buckley who suffers; and I have no solace for him except to remind him that there are people who think that the baroque altar is the most beautiful thing in Chartres. We will rid the liturgy of vulgarization when we rid TV of it, and I urge Mr. Buckley to lend his talents to both areas. It is like the war against sin; you never win it, but you never really lose it either.

I am impressed by Mr. Buckley's appreciation of the majesty and mystery of the Latin. Notice that I am not impressed by the majesty and mystery, possibly because I know more Latin than Mr. Buckley. Where is all this good taste in Latin? I dedicated several years in the diligent reading of Latin literature from Plautus to Juvenal (omitting Ennius because we did not have a text and Persius and Martial for reasons which I should not have to explain to a Yale graduate), and it is not from superficial observation that I say that never was so much inferior literature produced by so few. I carried this interest into the

Latin Fathers and the medieval theologians; and I have to say that you do not know what the words "dead language" mean until you see a dead language used in a living society.

If the *Dies Irae* which Mr. Buckley found so touching were sung in English, most people would leave the church; the poem is simply awful in form and content, and Horace would turn over in his grave if he heard it. Doesn't the *sense* of the words mean anything? If all that moves us is mystery and awe set to music, the hymn could be sung in Swahili with no perceptible loss. The great danger to the *Dies Irae* and many other Latin hymns is that they might be understood. But if words are no more than vehicles for musical notes, we could sing la-di-da just as well. Some choirs have been close to it for years. Majesty and mystery, my foot. Apparently Mr. Buckley has never seen a full-dress, solemn high show put on anyway but well. Let us from the hinterlands tell him that when it is fouled up, it beats anything he ever agonized through at St. Mary's.

The laity do not understand the English any better than they did the Latin. A valid point, Mr. Buckley; but do we then give up and go back to the Latin? Is it not possible that the translations will improve once we get some time to improve them? The affair was done hastily because it should never have been necessary to do it. The Protestants seem to find the vernacular a satisfactory medium, even if, at times they are a bit too Elizabethan for my taste. I do not blame the Authorized Version for sounding like Shakespeare—they were contemporaries—but I do not expect Mr. Buckley to sound like Shakespeare. It seems impossible for most translators of Latin to make their renderings sound like anything but English translated from Latin, although we are getting away from "Vouchsafe, O Lord" and "O God, who didst deign to conjoin in the angelic youth Aloysius a marvelous spirit of chastity with an incredible practice of penance." (What could be better conjoined, I might ask?) It does not have to be done in that way. Some of the trouble is in that original Latin which Mr. Buckley admires so much as long as it does not come through.

Because the laity do not understand the English, Mr. Buckley assumes that they never will understand it. Apart from the possibilities of improved translations, this assumption is unduly pessimistic and it is made too hastily. The possibilities of understanding are there, and many of the laity understand it better than Mr. Buckley thinks. There are no possibilities of a general understanding of the Latin, and I conclude that Mr. Buckley thinks understanding is neither possible nor especially desirable. Let me refer him to St. Paul, who said, "If I sing in the spirit, let me also sing with my mind"—and I do not think that sentence is notably obscure.

Let us come to the last and most important point: that congregational worship distracts one from prayer. The question is whether worship is a social function or not. Mr. Buckley inherits a long tradition when he says that it is not; this tradition was called "devotio moderna" in the fifteenth century. I think it is Bernard of Clairvaux, somewhat earlier, who is credited with "O beata solitudo! Sola beatitudo," which I render roughly "O blessed solitude! Sole Blessedness!" (It scans better in English, but is just as idiotic.) When Mr. Buckley addresses God, he wants no unwashed multitude screaming off-key in his ear. But what he wants is not social worship; a church full of people at private prayer is not a social group, just as the passengers on a plane do not form a social group. The liturgy for Mr. Buckley is a background of *son et lumière* which stimulates devotion by its majesty and mystery; but if it becomes so audible that conceptual language is heard, it takes his mind off his prayer. There is no reason why we should build churches and fill them with people so that they can furnish a background for private prayer. Confound it, Mr. Buckley can address God anywhere; one impulse from a vernal wood will furnish just as nice a background, and it is much less trouble. Social worship does remind us very forcibly of our common humanity, and I suppose it can be just as disagreeable a reminder as a trip on the 7th Ave. subway. But you cannot escape it by staying off the 7th Ave. line.

Some people, Mr. Buckley, prefer social worship; and I suppose you are right in saying that we should not force it on you. Speaking for myself as candidly as Mr. Buckley spoke for himself, I have to say that the presence of God frightens and embarrasses me, and reduces me to timid silence (no one will believe this). I rarely can muster the courage to address him unless I can hide in a crowd of *schlemiels* like myself; I guess there is a vague hope that even omniscience will not pick me out of a crowd so quickly. The sentiment may be akin to the sentiment of Amos 6:9-10. I have a theologically unsound feeling that God is more committed to a crowd of us than he is to me personally, and that he will have to reject the whole crowd if he wants to reject me. It is for such as us that social worship exists; and I fear we have you outnumbered. Social worship is our security blanket; and since Arnold Lunn and his educated few are gentlemen by definition, they will show us the kindly tolerance which gentlemen always exhibit toward the lower classes. It does not necessarily mean that we like or cherish bad taste in social worship; I still think of the altar of Chartres in terms not entirely unlike those in which Hosea spoke of the altars of Israel. And if Mr. Buckley thinks he can escape bad taste by private worship, I should be glad to refer him to some monuments of private worship like the writings of Sister Josepha Menendez.

I conclude that Mr. Buckley's experience of the reformed liturgy has been uniformly and particularly unfortunate. My experience must have been more fortunate. Not long after the vernacular was introduced I attended a wedding of two young friends. The priest obviously did not like the vernacular, and the ceremony could hardly have been more unattractive if it had been in Latin. I have been at wakes where there was a more cheerful atmosphere. I have never married and have no plans for it, but I think the wedding ought to have a note of joy and good cheer—not the same as the wedding breakfast, but not totally different either, and certainly distinguishable from a funeral. It was my good fortune to attend another wedding where the priest relished the vernacular, where audience participation was vigorous and the singing was simple but good. The symbolism of the sacrament was so transparent that one could not miss it; and one did not pass from the church to the wedding breakfast with the feeling that one had left the sacred for the profane. The suitable mood was set in the religious ceremony, and the champagne seemed less secular—tasted better, too. It can be done, Mr. Buckley; and I assure you it will be done.

*Chapter Twenty-Five*

# THE FUTURE OF
# RELIGIOUS LIFE

UNFORTUNATELY, it continues to be pertinent to ask whether it is the desire of the Holy See and the hierarchy that religious life continue to exist in the church. I have previously touched on the problem of vocation and defection, but apparently I did not touch hard enough. If the religious life assumes a character which attracts no candidates and repels those who are already members, it does not make much difference whether the life does or does not present an ideal worthy of the effort. If no one is making the effort, the ideal will not be realized.

The answer to my question has to be affirmative, and with emphasis; of course ecclesiastical superiors desire that the religious life continue and flourish. But this desire, however sincere it may be, can be pursued without reference to certain concrete realities. The most concrete reality here is that no one can be compelled to enter religion or to remain in it. In this sense the desires of the members have something to do with the way in which the religious life is determined.

It is not yet time to push the panic button. The religious life has been threatened with extinction before, and the present crisis has not yet assumed menacing proportions. Philip Hughes, in his history of the English Reformation, studied the monasteries of Tudor times in detail with statistics. His conclusion was that if Henry VIII had not suppressed the monasteries, someone else would have had to suppress them; they deserved suppression. The sturdy Benedictine order has survived so many reforms and suppressions that only a historian of Benedictine monachism can enumerate all of them. The Society of Jesus was actually extinguished by pontifical decree. The Franciscan Order flew into fragments as soon as its founder had died. The Protestant Reformation and the French Revolution were both the causes of enormous casualties in religious communities.

If the present crisis differs from earlier crises, it is only in this; that religious life is not under attack from some hostile alien force; the present crisis is strictly an intramural Catholic fuss. This may be a substantial difference, but it is not clear that it is; so far we are dealing with a group all of whom wish that the religious life continue, but in earlier crises there were active groups who wished that it should not continue. The difference now concerns the form and shape of the religious life.

Here we are reminded of another feature of the history of the religious life: it has always exhibited the capacity to create new forms for new situations. We have already mentioned the Benedictine reforms. The oldest order in the church has been, in the last analysis, the most flexible. I suppose there has not been an age in the church when the Benedictines were not "modern." But when the church had needs which the monks could not meet, the orders of the friars were created to do what the monks within their rule could not do. When needs arose which the friars could not meet, the orders of Clerks Regular came into being; they have been the models after which most of the more recent "congregations" have been formed. The genius of Vincent de Paul discovered a way in which religious women could become actively engaged in the work of the church. Two things should be noticed about each of these major developments in the religious life. The first is that each one of them was a change in the direction of greater freedom, and therefore a break with the "traditional" religious life. Secondly, each of them was accomplished only after long and discouraging opposition on the part of ecclesiastical superiors. Ignatius Loyola, whose name has become synonymous with obedience, said that his Society would exist according to his Constitutions or it would not exist at all. To paraphrase Patrick Henry, others may profit by his example.

This may suggest that we are on the eve of such another movement as those which produced the friars and the Clerks Regulars; and the church seems to need nothing less than new communities. My graduate assistant spent several tedious hours simply ascertaining the number of communities of men and women; even the *Annuario Pontificio* does not tot them up. Yet religious themselves resent the suggestion that they are so much alike that communities could be merged. Anyone who cannot see the differences in rule, in spirit, in work, and up to this time in habit, is kindly dismissed as not very perceptive. But a survey of the group as a whole leads one to wonder how many communities have been founded to do the work which another older community had been founded to do but was no longer doing. For instance, most teaching communities were founded to teach the children of the poor. How interesting. It seems to be the fact that it has been easier to found new communities in the church than to change old ones.

Until recent times—the last year or two—no groups in the church or in the world cherished archaisms as jealously as religious communities. The casual observer wonders whether this is any longer true at all. The archaisms had much in their favor. They contributed to the community identity—that is, you could tell one community from another by which archaisms each preserved. For one, it might be funny hats, for another no shoes, for many, rising at an ungodly hour suitable only for farm hands. More than that, the archaisms kept the communities predictable. Prelates could deal with them in the assurance that they knew what the religious wanted and what they did not want. We should understand the present prelatial uncertainty. What many religious want now, and the number seems to be growing, is to become the new orders which the age demands instead of letting someone else institute new communities. This is brand new in the government of the church, and a decree of the Second Vatican Council is not enough to put it over. I have noticed in many of my contemporaries a tendency to give the decrees of an ecumenical council a force which candidly they have never had in the church.

In our crisis the basic and most subtle archaism is that the traditional religious life does not recognize the "subject" as a person. This is the theory, however loose the practice may be. It is behind the usual abandonment of one's name; and we observe that the self-assertion implied in the use of one's personal name is becoming more and more common. It is behind the traditional obedience, in which all decisions are made for one by another. I have observed that when bishops become interested in something I do, it is the practice of most of them to communicate with the provincial superior, more rarely with the superior general. They cannot communicate with me because it is assumed I have no power of decision; it would recognize me as a person, and would make no more sense than communicating with an infant. If you are dealing with another's children, you talk to their parents, not to the children. Hence long discussions can ensue on the ethereal level of government and decisions made on that same level which are not communicated to the subject until the final decision is reached.

Something has happened in the world which makes this archaism less tolerable than it once was; and this is the development of personal freedom in Western countries. Religious obedience was not so extraordinary in the sixteenth century as it seems to us. Secular authorities, when they wished it, could and did exercise total control over the subject. Self-assertion did not mean much to the peasants and the craftsmen of older societies; it could be quite costly. I doubt that many religious really understand that which they accept until they have been in the community for some years. The ideal can be attractive only as presenting a genuine opportunity which cannot be realized except by the surrender of the person; and our younger contemporaries do not see this opportunity. They do not see it because it has not been presented to them; and the difficulty of presenting it may lead them to ask whether it is there to be presented. Perpetual adolescence must have more in its favor than it has been shown to have if it is to attract people as a way of life.

Many religious communities have never resolved the ambiguity whether they exist for the members or for the church. The ambiguity is not in the constitutions; no order or congregation has ever been founded except to serve the church. But a community is not known from its rules any more than the United States is known from its laws. There should be no problem in identifying the service of the neighbor with the spiritual good of the subjects. In fact, the service of the neighbor must be rendered according to the constitutions or it cannot be rendered. It will have to be rendered by some other community whose rules permit it or the neighbor will have to await the foundation of a new community with new rules. In the meantime he may starve or burn down Madison Street, but if the community renounces its traditions it has a real fear that it may not know who and what it is.

The ambiguity lies in the question whether the religious are more surely loving God by their domestic observances or by serving their neighbor according to his need. Obviously the observances are safer; they have been approved by the Holy See, but serving the neighbor according to his needs has not. The laymen can go out at night unaccompanied and encounter persons of the opposite sex without proximate spiritual danger; religious are made of more tender stuff. The layman can serve the neighbor even if he misses an hour of community prayer; for religious the community prayer is the only thing which charges him up enough to serve the neighbor. Our younger contemporaries are drawing conclusions about the value of serving the neighbor and the state of life in which it can best be done.

Because the church needs religious, and because the religious life has historically shown such vitality, I personally have no doubt that the necessary changes will occur. There are still enough people with the temper of the original founders left; they have the vision and the courage to do what must be done.

They should not expect any better luck than the founders, and no less success. Like earlier changes, these will be changes in the direction of greater freedom, and they will be stoutly resisted. But they will happen. Most people remember the name of Ignatius Loyola; very few recognize the name of Cardinal Caraffa. Let us leave him in the decent obscurity which history has assigned him, and in which other cardinals will join him.

*Chapter Twenty-Six*

# NOT ONLY PRESENT,
# BUT INVOLVED

**N**OT LONG AGO Norman Mailer's *The Armies of the Night* was thrust into my hands with a suggestion that it might furnish material for an article. It is irrelevant that this donation was made in response to a veiled threat to write on the theology of my cat Cesare. I happen to be Cesare's god, and I am beginning to think his theology is sounder than mine. Anything to avert this is legitimate, so I have read Mailer's book; and it does furnish food for reflection. I am a bit ashamed to confess to my literate readers that this was my introduction to Mailer. I was, being unacquainted with his work, somewhat surprised to find that Mailer can write; and that sympathy arose which always arises among those who respect language, whatever be the differences which divide them.

Mailer has a tendency to overwork the Anglo-Saxon monosyllables which deal with procreation and evacuation; let this be a piece of archaic narrow-mindedness in me, but I have always thought that these words have a limited if effective use, more effective when spoken than when written. On the printed page they give the reader the feeling that he has wandered into a public toilet. When Vietnam is ablaze and the streets of American cities may be the next to burn, one cannot seriously believe that it is a basic liberty, worthy of serious dedication, to be free to print the four-letter words. Mailer does not need them, and he ought to leave them to writers who do not have his skill.

Mailer's book, as everyone knows by this time, is a report of the October rally and march on the Pentagon. The first part, the novel, is a complete reconstruction of Mailer's part in the affair, with a full description of his thoughts and feelings. The second part, the history, is much shorter and attempts to narrate the events from the original planning to their conclusion on Sunday. Mailer says that the history of this affair will never be written; no one has given a detached report. This, however, is true of a great deal of history; and Mailer acknowledges this. But the historian who does find his way through a mass of prejudiced witness must himself be remote enough from the event to feel no deep passion. I say deep, for it is impossible to study even something as remote as the history of Sumer and Akkad without taking sides at some point in the history. But the choice which the student makes about his ancient heroes and villains is not as personal to him as the choice which he makes between Johnson and Goldwater. I agree with Mailer that the "facts" will not be ascertained in our time; and we might remember that there is still some obscurity about the details of the battle of Gettysburg.

One reviewer has said that Mailer exaggerates the importance of the incident. This is hard to judge; Mailer communicates the feeling—shared, I am sure, by most of those present— that he was a part of a historic occasion. Since he was in the front line and got himself arrested rather early in the proceedings, he missed most of the excitement. The feeling that one is not only present at the making of history but involved in it is rare; I have never had it, and most of those who are present are usually too busy to think about the historic importance of the occasion. The march took so long that it afforded ample time for meditation. Mailer is candid about himself; he is quite clear that he was stewed to the gills the night before, but by the time he was in the march he was cold sober. What began in levity ended in one of the most serious moments in his life.

What gave the event the high tragic seriousness? For Mailer, it was a confrontation of the genuine liberal with the establishment—"corporation land," he calls it; and it was the first serious

confrontation, with the prospect of a bloody head for the con-
fronters. Mailer is the very type of the alienated middle-class
liberal. He came from his bourgeois apartment where he writes
his books for bourgeois readers who pay their bourgeois dollars
for them to join some of his fellow bourgeois in rebelling against
the society without which they could not live. Mailer is serious
about Vietnam, but Vietnam is really a symbol. The painful
self-flagellation of the liberal when he contemplates the horror
of Vietnam would find another occasion if Vietnam were lacking. The self-flagellation is done because the liberal feels helpless, indeed bought and enslaved by what he hates. The march
gave him a chance to shake his fist at the establishment, but
about all it achieved was a shaking of the fist.

One of Mailer's more frightening insights is the potential for
fascism in our institutions. Others have voiced this insight—
Thomas Merton, for example, who could write about contemporary problems with the detachment possible only for those
who live in places like the hills of Nelson County, Kentucky.
(Yes, I have been there.) We do like to think of fascism as
something German or Italian or Spanish, but not American.
The response of the government to protests still falls short of
fascism; but if a fascist government were formed, Dean Rusk
and General Hershey would have to change practically no
thought patterns to serve in it. Mailer's further insight is that
the latent fascism is closest to the surface precisely in those
places which are "the real America"—the small towns, the
county seats, the rolling countryside. I have to hand it to the
boy from Brooklyn here, who probably has as much experience
of places like Paoli and Jasper as I have of Flatbush and Ja-
maica. I would like to assure Mailer that I think he is absolutely right; and General Hershey is, like me, a native of Indiana. Fascism is possible wherever there are Eichmanns.

Now I come to the meat of the question. If it were simply
a question of the good guys vs. the bad guys, one could make
an unclouded judgment. It is not; and both the establishment
and the liberals have committed this simplification. Demonstration has become a way of life nowadays; but your true nonvio-

lent does not plan a demonstration which will of set purpose include violence, nor does he provoke others to violence. He says his piece, which the Constitution guarantees him, and goes home. When the violent confront the violent, the good and bad causes become a shady gray; and I include under violence attacks on property, which is not as sacred as the human person but deserves some respect. The police and the military who are stationed to protect the property remain there because a threat worse than a club in the head awaits them if they desert. Mailer points out that one of the things which surprised the demonstrators in the eyeball confrontation was the discovery that the men in uniform were like themselves—young and frightened. But the police and soldiers were under discipline; the demonstrators were not. God forgive me for seeing no heroism in screaming obscene taunts at men who will be put in the stockade for responding, just as I see no heroism in those who finally are goaded by the taunts to use their superior force. The whole thing is an exercise in irrationality.

Nor, while we are on the subject, do I see how the cause of peace and justice is advanced by casual fornication on the Pentagon lawns. I see no big thinking in a planned invasion which at best can do no more than scare a few civil service secretaries out of their wits. This does not reach the establishment; I admit that no easy way has been found to reach the establishment, but one does not conquer irrationality by more irrationality. I read that Secretary McNamara watched the proceedings from his office window. The demonstrators had no hope of reaching him; and this is no reflection on his personal courage. Believe me, had I been Secretary of Defense I would have been at home watching the affair on TV. Whom were the demonstrators trying to reach? What did they hope to accomplish? Had they broken into the Pentagon, what more would they have accomplished? Eugene McCarthy, by the exhibition of a different type of courage, accomplished more single-handed toward the demonstrators' objective than all those who were carted off to the local calaboose. That he needed this demonstration before he could act is not at all clear. It would compromise his cause, which was the cause of civil rational discourse. The demonstrators cooperated with the establishment in destroying discourse.

Mailer judges the demonstration to be ultimately a failure. He thinks that it failed because the planning was split between the radicals and the moderate pacifists, who would not cooperate with anything which would lead to violence. The rally was for the moderates, the march for the radicals. When one is against something one cannot always choose one's company; when one is for something, selection seems easier. There is probably a law here which I do not have time to formulate. Had it been a purely radical affair, the numbers would have been smaller and I suspect the police and military clubs would have swung sooner and longer. Mailer is not the only reporter to attest the brutality of the expulsion; and brutality is not excused because "they asked for it." No one asks for brutality except for brutes, and it is only from brutes that one gets it. My point is that everyone came out of the affair with a dirty nose; but I suppose this is true of most human transactions.

I would not put the failure on poor planning and lack of unity. There can be no objective for such a demonstration except to move the establishment. The objective of massing 50,-000 people who would go to this trouble to protest the war *might* move the establishment. The radicals really did not want to move the establishment, probably because they think it cannot be moved. All they wanted to do was to spit in its eye; and the response of the establishment to this gesture was predictable. They fell to its level and rolled in the same gutter.

Mailer makes it reasonably clear that many were motivated by mindless hatred and fear. For all our fine talk about respect for persons, we depersonalize the establishment. By turning it into a thing we make it moral to scream and hiss at it, to deface its walls, to curse its employees. We also make it impossible to talk to it. Mailer's liberals are further from negotiations with the establishment than the establishment is from negotiations with North Vietnam, and basically for the same reasons. Each side wants to destroy the other. Reviewing the whole affair, I feel nothing but acute discomfort at living with so many self-righteous people, both in the establishment and in the radicals. Mailer's most frightening disclosure is the revelation of the polarized antihuman hatred which is creating a schism within us. We are being led to a choice between two opposed and total systems of political morality, each rooted in a messianic consciousness which permits no discussion or dissent.

## Chapter Twenty-Seven

# ANOTHER "GALILEO CASE"

B Y CHARISMATIC timing I left for a month's vacation in various western states only a few days before the publication of *Humanae Vitae*. I thought I deserved the vacation and I regard it as a constitutive element of a genuine vacation that one get out of touch as far as possible. Had I foreseen the events, I would have headed for the Northwest Territories. I was seated comfortably in the home of a friend in Colorado, sipping a refreshing beverage and congratulating myself on my foresight, when the telephone rang. My host announced with a puzzled look that the call was for me. The caller identified himself as a reporter for a national journal. "I know what you want," I said, "but how did you track me down?" He observed that it had not been easy. I gave him the desired statement a few days later, after he had sent me the text of the encyclical. By that time it had become impossible to say anything new, and it is impossible now. I write on the topic only because it will save time demanded for explaining why I do not. Let me expand on the brief statement given to the press so that I can join those who stand up to be counted. The press statement was not really made off the top of my head. Most of us had, consciously or unconsciously, been forming a response to what it seemed we must expect. The statement of the 87 theologians was drawn up quickly but not hastily; as a theological document it was at least as polished as *Humanae Vitae*.

My press comment was that the encyclical is another Galileo case and that it will destroy the moral leadership of the Papacy at least for a couple of centuries. These are the points to be expanded. That it is another Galileo case means that the encyclical takes a stand against a wide consensus; but the consensus here is wider than the consensus in the Galileo case, and it deals with morality, not with dogma. The consensus is nearly universal outside the Catholic Church, and everything indicates that it is shared by a majority of members of the Catholic Church. The projection is that the encyclical will, like the Galileo declaration, be widely ignored, and that the moral consensus will not be altered by the papal announcement. It is further probable that just as the church has never reversed its declaration on the Galileo case, so it will never reverse *Humanae Vitae*. The encyclical will simply perish with the erosion of time, but more quickly than the Galileo declaration perished.

These remarks indicate why it seems that the encyclical will destroy the moral leadership of the papacy for a long time; and the consideration of this probability leads to some of the grey areas of theology which must be studied more profoundly. The scope of this column permits no more than a recital of the problems, and such a recital must of necessity appear superficial. Superficiality is out of place in this question, and I am well aware that some critics will be alert to notice anything which appears superficial. The moral consensus mentioned above shows that the document imposes a doubtful obligation as certain; and no theological reasoning confers this authority on the Pope. There is another factor involved in this which not many have yet noticed, to my knowledge. The teaching office of the church, the overworked *magisterium,* means the authority of the church to proclaim the gospel. No theological source discloses any authority of the church in philosophy. The encyclical is based on the natural law, which means that it is based on philosophical reasoning. With no commission to teach philosophy, the church can speak on philosophy with no more authority than its philosophical reasoning commands. Philosophical reasoning is missing in the encyclical; but even if it were present, it would still not carry that weight which is attached to "authoritative" teaching in the proper sense—that is, it would not be "ecclesiastical" teaching. This does not imply that the Pope and other churchmen must be silent on philosophy; it does mean that they are not speaking from the *magisterium* when they discuss it.

It is possible, of course, to argue by philosophical reasoning to a conclusion which is in contradiction to belief. Most heresies fall into this category. The church rejects such conclusions by reaffirming and interpreting the gospel. If it also engages in philosophical disputation with the heretics, it moves to their level and speaks only with the authority of its reasoning. It has no commission to write the correct philosophy, although, to repeat, it does not thereby exceed its commission; and this is not as paradoxical as it seems. The church may not be able to meet the problem without engaging in philosophical discourse; my point is that it cannot engage in such discourse with the same assurance with which it proclaims its belief.

I have said that the encyclical does not employ philosophical reasoning, and it is not necessary to expand on the reasons which make the conclusion doubtful. To take one example from many, I cannot improve on the statement of the 87 theologians. I shall add only that the practical effect of the encyclical is to impose continence on millions of married couples. The encyclical seems unaware or unconcerned that this is an obligation of habitual heroism. Such an obligation, which makes the rare and the exceptional the rule of daily life, must be supported by argument of unusual strength beyond all doubt. Since the question was posed in terms of the natural law, such arguments are not only suitable, they are absolutely demanded. They have not been given.

The basic reason why the encyclical will destroy the moral leadership of the papacy is that the encyclical is an abuse of the teaching authority; and authority which is abused forfeits respect. Here we enter one of the grey areas of theology; we have no theology which deals with the abuse of the teaching authority. It is not a question of whether the authority can be and has been abused. Some of my colleagues have collected a number of exotic samples of pontifical statements which have been locked in the closet of family skeletons. No one now denies that they were errors; but how long must one wait to recognize an error? One forgives error; one does not so easily forgive its imposition.

We have no theology of abuse of the teaching authority because we have no theology of the ordinary teaching authority. Even the extraordinary or infallible exercise of authority is not clearly defined; "faith" and "morals" are still ambiguous terms. The Galileo case was justified under "faith" because the Bible says the earth is flat—and, I may add, the Bible never reveals any other view of the earth. "Morals," as I have attempted to show, must have some reservations if we are speaking of philosophical morality. The question is whether the church itself knows the limits within which it can teach with authority; the evidence from history is ample that it has not always recognized these limits. If the church does not know them, who does?

A Vatican spokesman was quoted in the press as saying that the encyclical is not infallible. It has never been ecclesiastical style to add to a document that it is or is not infallible; one wonders why this statement was made. Paraphrase: it can be wrong. Add: you had better believe it anyway. This seems to illustrate as well as anything else the lack of a theology of the ordinary teaching authority. A question is either open or closed; the statement seems to mean that it is not closed, but not open. This is somewhat parallel to the remark of an earlier Vatican spokesman that the church is not in doubt, it just moves from one certainty to another. Such remarks add to the difficulty of taking pontifical statements seriously.

The phrase used in official documents and in theological writing to describe the attitude of the Catholic toward the ordinary fallible teaching authority is "internal religious assent." It is internal as opposed to mere external submission, "obsequious silence"; it is religious because it is motivated religiously and not from the perspicacity of the proposition. Internal religious assent is not imposed upon anyone who is sincerely convinced that he knows better; but from him external submission is required, at least as far as public discussion is concerned. It is presumed by theologians who treat this that no one will be excused from internal religious assent except professional theologians whose studies may have been extensive in the area in question. But in questions of morality, experience also ought to be a factor. Those who have collected the examples of some egregious papal blunders of the past may not have noticed that most of them deal with moral questions, not dogmatic questions. A study of these might disclose how much failure to consult experience had to do with the blunders. In the present instance the experience of married life had no perceptible influence on the composition of *Humanae Vitae*. Experience, as well as theological research, is a factor in forming an internal religious assent to a pontifical document.

The theory behind internal religious assent is that the membership of the church is not equipped to settle theological problems; when the problems reach sufficient magnitude, it is the office of the church to tell its members what they must believe and do. The theory is basically sound, but there are two remarks to be made about it. One is that the theory easily develops into imperialism, and becomes an assumption not only that the members are not equipped to discuss theological problems, but that they cannot and should not equip themselves to do so. When this is extended to personal moral decisions, the imperialism begins to show. The second remark is that the office of the church implies a duty to do the work required to tell the members accurately what they should believe and do, and to give the necessary explanation. The encyclical does not show this work.

Some, I understand, feel gladdened that the Pope has effectively destroyed his moral influence. They think that this is the best thing he could have done to destroy the absolute monarchy of the papacy. I cannot share this joy. In the structure we know, the Pope is a spokesman for the church as no one else can be. The moral influence of the whole church is weakened when the papacy is muffled. No doubt the structure can be modified to meet this need; after all, the church was effectively without a Pope from 1377 to 1414, and it survived. No one would say that it was strengthened by this experience. It has known other periods when the papacy was so weak that it was meaningless; we learn from this that the life of the church does not depend on the papacy. But in the modern church the Pope has become a figure of world influence who is heard and respected. At the moment nothing appears to replace what is lost.

How will the papacy recover its moral leadership? Not, it seems, by a renewed theology of the ordinary teaching authority, nor by a decentralization of the Roman Curia, much as these things are needed. The papacy will recover its moral leadership in the only way in which Jesus Christ empowered it to lead, and that is by suffering. People demand this in their moral leaders; they do not see it in the papacy. What is most notably lacking in *Humanae Vitae*, even more than philosophical reasoning, is compassion. Those who lack compassion can learn it only by suffering, if by suffering; too often they learn nothing but self-pity. Because the church is the presence of Jesus Christ in the world, it will recover its moral leadership in the world, whatever the price its members must pay for it. It is the church which must suffer, not only the papacy.

*Chapter Twenty-Eight*

# THE INFALLIBILITY SYNDROME

**M**AN BITES DOG" becomes as routine news as obituaries compared to a Roman Catholic bishop who writes a book denying the doctrine of infallibility. The noteworthy prelate is the Most Rev. Francis Simons, Bishop of Indore in India, and the book is *Infallibility and the Evidence* (Templegate). I may suggest that if the Catholic Church has sees in Siberia, Bishop Simons could expect to be transferred there. It is interesting to a theologian that the bishop argues from a rather fundamentalist view of the New Testament in asserting that the New Testament gives no basis for the doctrine. It is interesting because even slightly fundamentalist interpretation never leads to a conclusion like this, also because a slightly fundamentalist interpretation is more likely to be grasped by the defenders of infallibility than a more critical interpretation. Interpreters of the New Testament have known for a long time that infallibility has no biblical basis, and I do not know why we have so rarely said so. Perhaps we thought that it would make no difference if we did.

The Bishop's thesis is that the New Testament gives us the only certainty we need and the only certainty we can get, and this is "moral" certainty. The New Testament neither guarantees an infallible authority nor shows any need for one. Many writers have been calling for a "reexamination" of many doctrines, of which infallibility is only one. Here is the re-examination, done by the bishop of Indore, and how many of you, like me, have to get out the atlas to find Indore? Do not bother; it is a city of 310,859 in the state of Madhya Pradesh, as far as I can make out; Rand McNally's boundaries are vague at this point. The conclusion of his reexamination is that there is no doctrine—surely as much renewal as anyone could wish.

The bishop embarrasses me; I have acquired a reputation as a fairly radical theologian, but I have learned to live with the doctrine of infallibility. Perhaps I am a crypto-conservative; but before this unpleasant conclusion is forced upon us, let me explain how I lived with the doctrine. I have come to think of infallibility in these terms: the church, and only the church, can pronounce with assurance what the church believes. I accept the Roman Pontiff as a vehicle of infallibility, because the Roman Pontiff alone in the church is empowered as an individual to speak for the whole church. When he speaks, he announces what the church believes, not what he believes, otherwise there is hardly room for infallibility. I limit this to belief, and do not extend it to "doctrine," whatever that may mean; the First Vatican Council spoke of faith and morals, and I am satisfied with the ambiguity of these terms. As I hope to point out below, one has to keep them ambiguous. Therefore neither the church nor the Roman Pontiff can speak infallibly of philosophy, history, law or literary criticism; these are not included in what the church believes.

The flaw in this understanding, of course, is that it does not imply that what the church infallibly professes as its belief is infallibly true. I understand the church as an infallible source of its belief in the same sense in which I am infallible source of my belief; no one else is better able than I to state what I believe. This means that my faith in the church rests on something besides its claim to infallibility. As far as I am concerned, I certainly do repose my faith on something else. I believe the Roman Catholic Church is an authentic continuation of that group which first appeared as the disciples of Jesus. I believe that this continuity can be historically established. In this ecumenical age I am now ready to accept the statement that the Roman Catholic Church does not have an exclusive claim to continuity; but it is the church in which I was reared and in which I live, and which I understand better than any other church. I see no other Christian body which assures me that it has a more authentic continuity, if "authentic" admits more and less. This sums up a great many things rather briefly, but we shall have to be brief in the space available.

The bishop has brought some of the hidden rationalization of my belief into the open. Actually I know that my own explanation of infallibility would not satisfy Roman theologians; and we do not know whether it is still important that they be satisfied. Theologians are aware of the rationalizations of infallibility. The church and the pope are not infallible unless they speak solemnly, *ex cathedra,* to the whole church, and concerning faith and morals. If one of these conditions fail, the teaching is not infallible. This leaves ample room for error. Historically, the Roman Catholic Church has needed all the room for error it can get.

Nobody outside of the professional theological world knows how many things the church has taught which we know were wrong. Perhaps they may not have been recognized as wrong at the time; but if an infallible authority means anything, it should mean the ability to transcend limitations of time and space, or at least the ability to say nothing when it is not sure of itself. One needs no charisms to enjoy this type of prudence. At one time the church burned heretics and preached holy war against the Moslems. What does it mean if we say that the church reflected contemporary *mores,* or that it never *taught* such practices, or that it did not teach them solemnly *ex cathedra?* These distinctions meant little to the heretics who burned and the Moslems who were massacred; and I have a stubborn belief that no human life is more sacred than any other human life, and that to use the life of the human person is a sin which cries to heaven for vengeance.

Other examples could be adduced, and have been adduced, particularly in connection with *Humanae Vitae.* Anyone who knows of a pontifical blunder in teaching now feels he should quote it. The supply is ample. The style of pontifical prose is so turgid that a simple dispensation for marriage sounds like the promulgation of the decalogue on Sinai. There is no doubt about the impression which these documents are intended to create. When do we reach a point where we recognize that when everything is solemn, nothing is solemn? The documents are so composed as to lead the faithful to believe that they are infallible until they are proved wrong. A teaching authority which claims infallibility and maintains a quick exit for all its errors would elsewhere be judged arrogant and dishonest. After all, I too am infallible when I am right.

The theology of infallibility, even as it is understood in conservative theology, means that the church is not infallible in its normal fulfillment of its teaching office. Then why claim infallibility? A teacher who admits that he can be in error is not claiming infallibility; and the church historically has not exhibited infallibility. We need not go all the way back to the prohibition of interest and the Crusades. In the twentieth century the Pontifical Biblical Commission issued a number of decrees about the literary criticism of the Bible. This commission is the only body in the world which settles problems of criticism by decree. Not one of these decrees is honored in contemporary biblical scholarship, and no one is censured for ignoring them. Yet they were proposed with some solemnity, and they restrained Catholic biblical scholarship for forty years. They were wrong and we know it. I do not ask why they were issued; even a Pontifical Commission has a right to express its opinions. But why were they not delivered as opinions? That is all they were. They have not been reversed or withdrawn; the infallibility syndrome forbids the Catholic Church to admit that its teaching bodies were ever wrong. We never learn that a teaching of the church is in error from the church itself.

Now the standard evasion for the blunders of the Biblical Commission is that the Commission is not the supreme teacher and that it cannot speak solemnly; nor did it deal with faith and morals. But it did speak; men were suspended and dismissed from teaching because they did not accept it. Then why did it speak at all, if it did not speak as the supreme teacher in a solemn manner? Why did it not simply shut up? The infallibility syndrome is a symptom, not a disease. The disease is the compulsion to impose doctrine upon the faithful, to control thinking and expression. It has now become manifest that the Roman Curia is incapable of speaking for the whole church; it is not even in touch with the whole church, and theologians know that it is completely out of touch with theology. Yet it seeks to impose—what? Not faith and morals, certainly. What is sought is power; and the lust for power needs no explanation here which would be different from an explanation elsewhere. It is pleasant to have power, and no one needs to explain why he wants it.

I keep saying until I get tired of saying it and others get tired of hearing it that the church is empowered in the New Testament to proclaim the gospel and not to do anything else. If infallibility is meaningful at all, it can only be meaningful here; and it may mean no more than the assurance that the church never loses the gospel. But the church can certainly foul up its proclamation, because it has done so. It can proclaim other things besides the gospel, and it can claim infallibility for them. It can continue to claim infallibility even after error is demonstrated. If infallibility is thought to mean that the faithful have security in faith and morals, forget it; infallibility has never meant that and does not mean it now. When we ask what infallibility does mean, we may find that it means nothing.

Yet it seems impossible to say that it means nothing. Perhaps my understanding of the church as a sure source of its own belief has more in its favor than one would think. If this is what is meant, "infallibility" says too much. If the word must be retained, the reservations on its meaning are so severe that it ceases to be the apt word. The church must offer some spiritual security that other agents do not offer. The doctrine of infallibility is not a good expression of this security. The word has acquired unsavory connotations of control which, as several commentators have pointed out, are more suggestive of Communist orthodoxy than they are of the church of the New Testament. Some other term should be sought for what the church wishes to say. "Infallibility" is calculated to project an image which does not correspond to the reality.

It may not be a revision of dogma which is needed, nor even a revision of theology. The end which is sought could be achieved by a more modest style of church teaching, whether the source is the pope or the bishops. How the prelates love to thump! If they were to accept the obligation which lies upon us "little men," to borrow a phrase from an undistinguished prelate, of presenting evidence for their conclusions, of confessing doubt where there is doubt and of probability when that is all they have, if they were to attempt persuasion rather than coercion, if they were open to objection and criticism, it is altogether likely that the teaching office of the church would enjoy more respect than it does when it claims infallibility with a built-in escape for error.

The infallibility syndrome is an effort to attach divine attributes to the teaching authority. To predicate divinity of creatures is idolatry by definition. Should these more modest techniques be adopted, the teaching authority of the church would find that it spoke less frequently and on a much more limited variety of topics; we should not have allocutions to midwives given us as authentic sources of doctrine. The necessity of thought would arrest the flow of pronouncements, and the church might even hear the gospel proclaimed. It is too much to ask that our teachers be the least among us; but it seems reasonable to ask that they do not claim to be God.

## Chapter Twenty-Nine

# NEITHER SLAVE NOR FREEMAN, MALE NOR FEMALE

**I**T MAY SURPRISE the more vocal feminists, but some of us boys worry about the antifeminism in the church, too; and I think we ought to listen when they use ugly words about us. Only the Negro can tell us when we are anti-Negro, and only the Jew can tell us when we are anti-Jew; it would seem to follow that if women say we are antifeminist, the complaint is not answered by saying that some of my best friends are women, but I wouldn't want my daughter to marry one.

Give us a break, however, up to a point. I have read no major work on the modern feminine problem except Betty Friedan's, and I felt after reading her book I would be glad to support her in getting whatever it is she wants as soon as both of us know what it is. I do not say "giving" her because the very word is patronizing; it may not be in my power.

It is possible that their womanhood has impeded some women from reaching the fullness of their potential, but that gets no tears from this corner. Most of us are impeded by something. My scholarship interferes with my priesthood, and my priesthood interferes with my scholarship. You may say that I chose to be a priest but that women had no choice about being women, and there is no denying this; but we both had a choice of the intellectual life. In all good faith I entered into a double role for which there is ample precedent in the church, and it took much of my mature life to learn that the definition of these roles in the church of my generation is so ambiguous that it is extremely difficult to combine them. So it is difficult to combine womanhood with a professional career? Those who want something more than they can get sitting under a tree waiting for apples to drop have to work harder than the sitters. This is not to say that a great many women do not work harder; I am sure they do, and one of the things I do not know about the other half is how much harder it works.

We are talking about antifeminism in the church, and I have already said that I recognize it and that I do not believe in it. When I first began to arrange some thoughts on this thing, I intended to say that it is a cultural battle and not a theological battle. But we know now that the two are intermingled so deeply that any separation would be entirely artificial. Theology should influence culture and often does. St. Paul—who you girls think is the original Christian antifeminist—wrote that in Christ there is neither slave nor freeman, male nor female. The Christian world did not reject slavery until the nineteenth century, and I see no non-Christian influence which would have accomplished it. We are slower about women, but I would not give up. Biblical studies have driven me into ancient culture, and I found that in ancient cultures men owned women. The tribal view of women gave them a definite place which tribal women seemed and seem willing to accept; they were baby machines and housekeepers. They were also one of the few authentic pleasures in the dangerous and uncomfortable conditions of primitive culture. And tribal culture recognized women in its own peculiar way. Both the fertility goddess and the biblical etymology of the name Eve present woman as the symbol of life. This did not keep her from exploitation; and you could call the history of woman a history of exploitation. Much of the trouble is that women, being more realistic than men, learned not only to accept the exploitation but to enjoy it. It was the only way in which they could and did exploit the exploiters.

Are we past all that? Not on your life. Let us look briefly at the traditional Catholic theory of marriage as you find it in moral theology and in canon law. I sometimes refer to it as the breeding-pen theory of marriage. The woman appears as baby machine, housekeeper, and an authentic pleasure—to be enjoyed, however, with the greatest restraint. The theory is entirely male-directed; women, my dear, are not supposed to theorize about anything. We men do your thinking for you. You do not know what you want until we tell you. Have you ever noticed that in the marriage formula so long in use the word "love" does not occur? Love is not necessary in the breeding-pen theory. If you read the breviary, you might get a few chuckles out of it if you still have your sense of humor. The finest thing the church can say about some of its married saints, men and women, is that they never used their partners sexually. The paradox did not strike the writers of the nocturns. The finest Christian marriages in this book are those in which the partners pretended that they were not married. But the heroines in these stories do not even rise about the quaint classification of "Holy Women Not Virgins."

What I am trying to say, I suppose, is that it is not the church but the relics of tribalism in the church which offend you. In the academic, business and professional worlds, I am told, women are paid less than men for the same work across the board. This is tribal. It should be added that the tribal culture has survived longer and stronger in some Latin cultures which are closely associated with the church than in other countries; I refer you to the revealing book *The Italians* by Signore Luigi Barzini. Things may be worse than you think. I have already suggested that it is more than a theological battle, and I accept the implication that the church ought to lead the culture rather than follow it. This leads us to another and perhaps the most important strictly ecclesiastical factor in your problem, a factor which I say is also tribal.

This factor is celibacy. I am not talking about whether celibacy ought to be, but simply noticing some results of it as it has been and is. In spite of what you hear, most priests remain celibate. How do you think this is achieved? It is achieved by withdrawing young men just during their flaming years from all association with women and by a steady program of warning that women are dangerous. Now this is the tribal element. It is a part of masculine mythology that women are the weaker vessel, that women are oversexed and just looking for the next man. How well this prepares men to deal with women you can imagine, and I think it is a credit to most of us priests that we do quickly learn better. But not all of us do, and you will meet some who cherish a hostile fear of women all their lives. They know no other way to remain what they are supposed to be.

But the celibate loses none of his masculinity. In fact, since he denies himself one normal expression of the same, he may exaggerate other expressions. The Germans have a proverb: "Dreckig wie ein Mannerkloster." He certainly loses none of the masculine desire to dominate women; and the tribal culture presents the absolute ideal of masculine domination. Without enough women around to cut him down, his masculine ego can grow to intolerable proportions; and it is fed in addition by the fear that if he does not dominate he will be dominated.

So here we are dragging a tribal male-female culture into the twenty-first century. What you want, I suppose, is to be recognized as persons. In the tribal culture the only personal encounter of man and woman is the sexual encounter. Any relationship is presumed to lead to this. We have not yet learned that while a man can like many women—or all of them, if his tastes are broad enough—he can really love only one. And to be fair to us men, I think it should be noticed that many women are just as tribal as any man. A person is far more than a gender, but a person can hardly stop having a gender; it seems to be the way we are made. I do not suppose that women want to become men, and you can stop the world and let me off when they do. Nor do I suppose that women want to be recognized as persons apart from their womanhood. Do we have the theological and cultural framework for a kind of male-female relationship which is really quite new in the world? I am satisfied that we have the theological basis; but the culture frightens me.

*Chapter Thirty*

# THOSE WERE THE DAYS

IN THE FALL of 1924 I boarded a Pennsylvania Railroad
train, drawn by a K-4 steam locomotive, at the Union Station of Terre Haute, Indiana, for a trip of 550 miles which
terminated at St. Mary's College, St. Mary's, Kansas. Since
the Pennsylvania Railroad, the K-4, the Union Station and St.
Mary's College have all passed out of existence, that one sentence ought to have enough nostalgia for the week. St. Mary's
College closed its doors in June, 1931, not so much a victim
of the depression as of alienation from its culture.

St. Mary's was the St. Maure's of *Tom Playfair*, the most celebrated hero of the boys' book of Father Finn; my younger contemporaries will not believe how well known Tom and St.
Maure's were between 1900 and 1920. The baseball team
played an exhibition game with a professional team in the
spring of 1907 and beat the professionals; so, at least, our local
legend had it. The team was owned by a St. Mary's alumnus
who wanted to bring his players to his old campus. The alumnus was Charles Comiskey of Chicago and his team was the
White Sox, then the champions of the world after their stun-
ning defeat of the Cubs of Frank Chance (and Tinker and
Evers). Old St. Mary's had few days of glory on its athletic
fields other than that; its best game was baseball in a period
when college baseball was entering its permanent decline.
Yet there were left golden memories of a peppery little Irish-
man named Steve O'Rourke who migrated to the prairies from
Worcester, Mass., and Holy Cross College to coach all the sports

(that is how amateur we were) and teach an excellent and demanding course in fourth year high school English. It was there, and not in the sports, that I encountered him. One of his ball players once noticed that the umpire was not looking and scored from second base via the pitcher's mound. The screams of the opposition could be heard in Topeka, but the player would have gotten away with it had he not left a clear trail of spike prints across the diamond, still moist from the rainfall of the preceding night. We were never sure that Steve's heart was in the rebuke he administered; Steve was a competitor, and he was laughing.

I once told a colleague that the discipline of St. Mary's was medieval. The colleague, a competent historian of the Middle Ages, rejected the adjective as unfair to the Middle Ages. The school was founded in 1848 for Indians, and the discipline imposed upon the noble red youth of the prairies was more or less maintained long after the school had gone Caucasian. It was not merely that the students were routed—the word is not used figuratively—out of bed at 6:00 A.M. except on Sundays and holidays, when we slept late—6:30 A.M. The situation can best be grasped if one realizes that a student who could not be precisely and instantly located at any hour of the day or night was seriously out of order. This demanded constant supervision and complicated charts, managed by a large staff of Jesuit scholastics. We were put to bed at 10:00 P.M., and the bull switch was thrown at 10:10. Early to bed and early to rise gets damn tiresome very quick.

The village of St. Mary's in 1924 looked like a set from a William S. Hart movie; as I learned later, it was populated by good gentle people, and I have been in religious houses which offered about as much spiritual danger. There was hardly a thing to do there, good or bad, except to get off the reservation. Permission to do this could be granted once or twice a month for two to three hours. If you were a college senior you might get as much as one night a week. Enough village girls married students to suggest that the Jesuit wall was not as tight as they thought it was.

The class distinction between dormitory students and private room residents was odious then, and its memory is still odious; freedom was literally for sale. Dormitory students had no escape from four hours a day of silent supervised study in a large study hall. One who liked to read, and I did like it, could have made good use of this opportunity. But anything which was not obviously a classroom text would bring the prefect down on one. I suppose I resent this enforced waste of time more than anything else. I had a fairly good IQ, and the teachers were unable to assign work that I could not do in thirty minutes or less. I can still recite some pages from my textbooks. Some supervised reading would have been helpful; but while St. Mary's was generously staffed with men whose chief skill was managing other people's lives, the improvement of those lives on any but traditional terms was not in view. If the Jesuits did not invent the term *in loco parentis,* they certainly gave it full meaning—except that even in the 20s it would have been a rare parent who did not allow the young more liberty than we had. I suspect many parents wanted the restrictions, but preferred to have the Jesuits fink for them. By 1928 even the parents did not like to hear their young describe the old school in terms which suggested a prison, a reservation or the not yet existent concentration camp.

The education had been strictly classical, and it was just being modified. I have never been sorry for drill in the basics of Latin, Greek, English and history; I am sorry only that more was not demanded of quick learners. The teaching was not great, but it was, with very few exceptions, professional and dedicated. One of our principals, known familiarly as the Wild Bull of the Campus (an allusion to the then well-known Luis Angel Firpo, knocked out by Dempsey in something like two and a half minutes), perished in the hurricane of 1931 which destroyed most of Belize, British Honduras, and St. John's College with it. One of the survivors heard Bill leading his class in prayer as they went under water. That would be Wild Bill; and I ask those who find the story corny whether they have prepared any apt speeches in case they should find themselves drowning with the class they are teaching. These men were so professional and so dedicated that one could dislike very few of them in spite of the abominable disciplinary system which they faithfully administered. It used to be thought that so many vocations came from St. Mary's because novitiates and seminaries were fairly easy to take after some years of totalitarian supervision.

How did we like it, and how did alumni feel? Not too much should be made of the fact that the provincial superior who made the decision to close the school was himself an alumnus. The late Father Matthew Germing, as I knew him, made no decisions based on human feeling. We were like most boarding school students in those days: it was fashionable to hate the school on campus and to boast about it on vacations, and to boast about it precisely because it was so tough. The close quarters made for a peculiar kind of comradeship, as well as for some spectacular fights; these institutions had some features of the prison, the barracks and the forecastle. We had movies once a week (except in Lent, of course), varsity teams to watch, and an almost compulsory program of competitive sports. This last was something of a hardship on those less endowed with vision and coordination. The idea seemed to be to keep us too fatigued for mischief; and it did not work to perfection. We were young and healthy, and we could have written the sailors' chorus from *South Pacific*.

I am not sure I had many close friends, but there were a great many men of whom I have kindly memories. Some memories of another kind are fewer and less enduring. Since we had four years of high school and four years of college on the same campus, we had a kind of mix which I have not seen since. St. Mary's students would not tolerate the boy who was too good to talk to anyone. Such may have come, but they did not stay. Democratic we were, on social, economic, intellectual and athletic grounds; we were painfully antisnob.

Yet we had the defects of our society. One of the most famous figures of the campus was Thomas Goodall, employed by the college from 1905 until about 1930. He was the cook, and no St. Mary's man will fail to mention the cornbread. He was black, and I always thought accepted even if patronized; returning alumni used to look for Tom first, and then the president. I suppose the modern black would think him the very model Uncle Tom. I think of him as one of the five real gentlemen I have met in my life, whoever the other four may be. His oldest son worked in the kitchen while I was in school. I did not learn until a few years ago that Tom had wanted his son to go to school at the college as a day student. The authorities, in view of a fairly large southern enrollment, felt it would be unwise to accept him. Neither Tom nor his son ever said a word about this. Yes, we were lily white. It was at St. Mary's that I first encountered another form of native prejudice. Traditionally St. Mary's had a group of students from Mexico. Democracy stopped at the Mexican colony.

And now, where are they all? A defunct school has no focus for its always shrinking alumni. We did not produce any national figures. Occasionally I will encounter a name in my travels and wonder whether it is the same which I remember from St. Mary's. More and more rarely I meet one. Anyone who attended St. Mary's at all has to be over fifty. I wonder whether my schoolmates became permissive parents. I think I am a permissive teacher, and I suspect it is a rebound from the iron discipline of my adolescence. I last saw the campus four years ago, when it was still a theological seminary, which it became in 1931. It was like a visit to a graveyard. Ghosts were walking all over the place, the ghosts of the youth of the roaring Twenties who little knew what awaited them when they left St. Mary's. How well did St. Mary's prepare them for the world of the 30s and the 40s? How well did any school prepare its students for that world? Do younger contemporaries, when they look at the world we made between 1940 and 1970, think our schools did not prepare us well? There is little we can tell them except that it could have been worse; that no school can prepare its alumni for an unexpected economic collapse and an international political collapse; that in such moments of crisis it is wisdom and integrity which count, and no school has ever taught these. The best it can do is make its students sympathetic to them.

In at least one respect the traditions of St. Mary's rested on a false assumption. When the Jesuits finally closed out in 1968 they looked for a buyer of 1200 acres with a dozen solid institutional buildings. They have not yet found a buyer, but I am told that they invited the Kansas State Department of Correction to inspect the property. The Department did inspect, and regretfully judged it unsuitable for its purposes. Shucks, fellows, we always thought that was just what it was most suitable for.

## Chapter Thirty-One

# THE HISTORICAL JESUS
# OF SUPERSTAR

**N**OT LONG AGO I was persuaded by a friend to listen to part of the album, *Jesus Christ Superstar*. I was not too happy with the invitation for a couple of reasons. One was irreverence. Do not get me wrong; I have been a Catholic since baptism in infancy, and the irreverence shown to Jesus Christ in the Catholic Church has rendered me immune to shock. But I have never learned to enjoy irreverence. Another reason was that I felt distaste for those who make money off Jesus Christ, or thought I felt it. My feelings about this have since become mixed, as I shall shortly explain. It was, I believe, Mr. John Lennon of the Beatles who said once that his group was bigger than Jesus'. The remark was much misunderstood by the devout; all the same only Mr. Lennon's youth can excuse such a colossal mistake. Jesus Christ is easily the all-time champion moneymaker, with not even a close second worth mentioning.

As my friend assured me, the score was not what I expected. It was reverent in the sense that it took Jesus seriously. It had none of the distortions of the devotional Christ, who is often so phony with plaster, gilt, tinsel and goo that it is no wonder unbelievers flourish. The devotional Christ is totally incredible. We Catholics who scream about "the historical Jesus" are really the last people in the world with a right to scream, considering what we have done to destroy his historical reality. There is a moving picture about Jesus which I did not see and the name of which I forget, but one reviewer struck a sympathetic chord in me when he (or she) wrote that he (or she) almost retched in the aisle when the crucified Jesus revealed that his armpits had been shaved. I submit that this is blasphemy, and I am not sure that it was in good faith. It is on the same level of art as the Infant Jesus of Prague, against which I have been carrying on an unsuccessful guerilla war for years. Whatever the historical Jesus was, he was not effeminate, and I am sure that he looked much more like the late President Nassar than he did like Paul Newman—with no implication that Mr. Newman is effeminate, I hasten to add, but he has a different style of beauty. If the real Jesus tried to get into Holy Name Cathedral, the ushers would heave him across State Street. If he entered my apartment building, the management would call the cops. The historical Jesus? Who wants him? Who ever wanted him? When he did show up, they crucified him—and there is no specification in the word "they." In fact, a better pronoun would be "we."

This is, however, the Jesus of *Superstar*. He knows pain and fatigue—not the pain and fatigue of the body, but the pain and fatigue of the soul, the kind that hurts deep inside. He even knows uncertainty, the kind of uncertainty which the devout are compelled to deny him, in spite of some rather clear sentences in the Gospel of Mark. We interpret these sentences as if Jesus had said, "OK, now I am supposed to have an agony so let's go through it." He also knows the pain of bearing a responsibility which is literally too much for flesh and blood to stand, and there is not a living soul who even notices it. All of us, if we live long enough, come to know the loneliness of severe pain; *Superstar* knows that Jesus knew it too. The complaint may be made that the Jesus of *Superstar* is too human, but just how a man goes about being too human is hard to figure, unless we think he is just pretending and is overacting a bit.

I do not wish to imply that *Superstar* does a perfect job. I did, after all, hear only part of the score; I did not witness the entire production. I merely want to report my impression that what I heard showed a surprisingly sympathetic understanding of the historical Jesus, an understanding which many believers do not have and I fear do not want. They will cling to their manufactured plaster Jesus who neither feels pain nor inflicts it. To steal a phrase from Nietzsche, they have buried Jesus in the church. But he does rise, even from this tomb. Because *Superstar* looks for the real Jesus, not for the idol created by Christians, I say it is deeply and seriously reverent, and has a better chance of finding him than those who want a plaster Jesus instead of a real Jesus. You cannot use the real Jesus to shore up a power structure or an economic enterprise. He refuses to be window dressing for cheap religious merchandise. For religious purposes such as these he must be encased in plaster so that, like the idols of the Gentiles in the Psalms, he has eyes but sees not, ears but hears not, feet but walks not, and—most important of all—a mouth but speaks not.

I am hinting rather broadly that Catholics are idolaters— many of them, anyway; why hint? This is what I mean. I am saying that this dawned on me as I heard the *Superstar* score. I realized that the composers were trying, not without blunders, to find the real Jesus, and that most of my fellow Catholics would hate them for it. It is almost like, if you will pardon the expression, raising a dead man to life. Perhaps they did it poorly in *Superstar;* if I ever see the whole production, I will have an opinion on that. We churchmen do not try to do it at all. Jesus is a stage prop for the pageantry of the Roman Catholic Church. If it hurts any to read this, I hope it hurts a lot.

Now—since I really have two chapters in one—let us turn to the other theme, the exploitation of Jesus for profit. *Superstar* indeed! It is an excellent title. When I said thoughtlessly that I did not like to see people make money off Jesus, I felt a sudden discomfort, as if I had sat on a tack. It was almost one of those inner voices, and I know people who have had similar experiences and thought they were hearing Jesus. I know I was not, but the content was much in his style. The message was something like this: And you, Buster, who pays you for your teaching—more than it is worth? Those books, those lectures, those articles, your own private war on poverty, your efforts to keep McKenzie from becoming a depressed area—are not all these gainful employments of your spin-offs from the Christ event? Well, I plead with myself, I do work for a living at what are understood as lawful and socially acceptable activities; it is demanding and exhausting work, and did not Paul quote the Lord as saying that those who preach the Gospel should live from the Gospel? Ah, the little voice said with some exasperation, you are indeed a great scholar and words are your game; you always have an answer, and you get away before the questioner realizes he is knee deep in snow. The question was not whether what you do is lawful and socially acceptable (indeed, I will stipulate that you may be an event in the church of the twentieth century, although I doubt it); the question was whether you make money off Jesus Christ. And I see your answer coming, that you are no worse than anyone else and a damn sight better than some we could mention; just stick to the question. Since I always lose arguments with myself, I said what was proper to say: nothing. Very well, the little voice went on, then shut up about those who make money off Jesus Christ unless you want to talk about us.

Very well, little voice, let us talk about us. I do make money off Jesus Christ. The fact that I am in the company of Paul VI, Cardinal Cody, the University of Notre Dame, The Thomas More Association, the Will & Baumer Candle Co., the Toomey Shirt Co. and many, many others does not alter that statement.

It is hardly a thrilling theological discovery to learn that the church is a secular institution; but, like the Grand Canyon, it discloses something new at each visit. The admired response of Francis of Assisi to his insight is literally inimitable; it was authentic holiness, but it was a stunt, and Il Poverello in the last analysis was a saintly nut whom I would not trade for all the cardinals who ever lived. But how many saintly nuts can we stand? And a thirteenth-century answer is out of date.

Dorothy Day is more contemporary, and some people think she is saintly (if she ever reads this, she will never forgive me). More people think she is a nut. But she is one of the few of our contemporaries who solved the problem of working for Jesus without living off him in an offensive way. If you count the people who have shared her solution, it is clear that the only thing wrong with it is that very few people are big enough for it. And that is your problem, Miss Day; people of your spiritual dimensions are no damn good for us pygmies.

I talk about leadership so much it becomes tiresome. I confess I need leadership and company in meeting this problem. Asking official leadership to face the problem of living off Jesus is, I know, like hiring John Dillinger as security chief at a bank; but to steal a phrase from LBJ, it is the only official leadership we have. Even Francis of Assisi did not make a dent in it. I do, however, think it is the official leadership's office to proclaim the gospel. Let us hear them loud and clear on this part of it.

They have their problems, I have mine. It is simply not conceivable that Jesus ever meant to establish anything which would enable men systematically to exploit him for profit. It does not solve my problem to recognize that Jesus did not create the system in which I and others live off him, but it helps to bear it. I, of course, did not create the system. And do I have either the freedom or the power to change it or to withdraw from it? The same Paul who quoted the Lord about the support of the preacher said of himself that he did not use this option but earned his living at the quite secular trade of tentmaking. Paul was a part-time apostle and a full-time tentmaker. Even in his day that was not the apostolic routine, and one doubts very much that it could be done today. I and people like me are really full-time academics and part-time priests. We say that if it was good enough for Thomas Aquinas it is good enough for us.

Why the fuss, little voice, if the Lord did say that those who preach him can live off him? Perhaps it is that we live too well off him. There is an irrational and inarticulate feeling of guilt at the realization that Jesus could live as a Palestinian villager and do his work when I cannot so live and do mine. Certainly Jesus understands this; I do not understand it. A part of the guilt turns to terror at the thought that while I live off Jesus, I might not be doing his work. If this be the case, I am best defined as an industrious thief. We come back to where we were, that the church in which so many people live off Jesus is in this respect a quite secular economic enterprise which fulfills its purpose of supporting in something better than destitution those who work for it. Mother Church, Mother Bell? They both promise job security, promotion by seniority, and retirement pensions. The help will not work for anything else.

**DATE DUE**

| | | | |
|---|---|---|---|
| | | | |
| | | | |
| | | | |
| | | | |
| | | | |
| | | | |
| | | | |
| | | | |
| | | | |
| | | | |
| | | | |
| | | | |
| | | | |
| | | | |

239
M
**McKenzie, John L.**
AUTHOR

**Did I Say That ?**
TITLE

239
M
McKenzie, John L.
Did I Say That